CHRISTIAN THEATRE
A Handbook
for Church Groups

Sylvia Read *and* William Fry

Christian Theatre

A Handbook
For Church Groups

EYRE & SPOTTISWOODE LTD
London . England

First published in Great Britain in 1986
by Eyre and Spottiswoode Ltd,
North Way, Andover, Hampshire, SP10 5BE
Copyright © 1986 by Sylvia Read and William Fry
Printed in Great Britain

British Library Cataloguing in Publication Data

Read, Sylvia
    Christian theatre : a handbook for church groups.
    1. Liturgical drama 2. Christian drama
    3. Dancing–Religious aspects–Christianity
    I. Title   II. Fry, William
    264   BV10.2

    ISBN 0–413–80260–4

Contents

Preface

1 A new beginning 1
2 Religious Drama — what is it for? 5
3 Starting a drama group in your church 10
4 Drama in worship 16
5 Launching out on a play 22
6 The director's vision 30
7 Fitting it into the church 39
8 Do we have to have all these rehearsals? 48
9 The magic of the spoken voice 54
10 Getting into character 62
11 Acting — a form of loving one's neighbour 70
12 Backstage community 75
13 What are we going to wear? 81
14 Staging and setting 93
15 Let there be light 102
16 Noises on and off 112
17 Drumming up an audience 118
18 On the night 122
19 Where do we go from here? 126

Appendix: Voice Drama 131
Useful addresses 135
Further reading

Preface

by the Bishop of Winchester

For twenty-five years Sylvia Read and William Fry have in Theatre Roundabout toured the length and breadth of the United Kingdom, with occasional forays into Europe and the United States, presenting Christian plays, anthologies, and adaptations of classical dramas and novels. They have brought to their work a unique combination of artistic insight, theatrical professionalism, Christian commitment and an unquenchable enthusiasm to engage with the heart, mind and imagination of their audiences. In varying moods they tease and delight, provoke laughter and tears, and as they strip away what is false and trivial they enable us to reflect more deeply and compassionately on the truth of the human condition.

Their dedication to Theatre Roundabout has been selfless and sacrificial, a kind of heroism. They have presented over two thousand five hundred performances, sometimes in spacious cathedrals and great parish churches; more often in shabby church halls and Victorian churches woefully lacking in basic facilities which make for ease of production. Yet they have consistently shown that religious drama is worthwhile, that it can speak to all sorts and conditions of people, and that it is possible even in the most constricting circumstances to make a presentation that is intellectually and spiritually honest, artistically satisfying and enables an audience to enter into a life-enhancing experience.

Christian Theatre is a distillation of the authors' wisdom, knowledge and experience. It is a goldmine of information for those who are just beginning to get involved in religious drama, and it cannot fail to help and encourage actors and producers who already have some experience. Many will be grateful to the writers for their guidance not only in surmounting the problems and pitfalls which attend the production of plays in churches, but also for showing how a printed text can become alive in performance and interpretation. I hope that this book – and its authors – will enjoy a long life in the furtherance of religious drama.

Colin Winton
President of RADIUS
June 1985

A new beginning

Since the late twenties there has been a rising tide of religious drama. More and more churches regularly stage a Nativity Play; Passion Plays have been written or revived; the great mediaeval Mystery Cycles have been performed in theatres, cathedrals, ruins or even (as they originally were) on trundling carts; touring companies have presented programmes of Christian sketches; famous writers and directors have presented films and plays about the life of Christ; and the world of the popular musical was dominated for some years by *Godspell* and *Jesus Christ Superstar*. More recently, the National Theatre has presented a version of the mediaeval Mystery Plays, which went on to play to packed houses in the West End.

Sixty years ago there was almost nothing like this in Britain. Many church people regarded the theatre with the gravest suspicion, and the idea of telling the Christian story through drama seemed dangerously near the edge of sacrilege. The theatre was prevented from being religious by the same laws that prevented it from being obscene.

The movement has grown so suddenly that it is easy to forget that religious drama is nothing new. It is certainly as old as theatre, a great deal older than literature, and possibly as old as religion itself. The classical drama of ancient Greece developed from the primitive rituals of the threshing-floor. The tribal dances of Africa, now being swept away, are certainly a form of religious theatre. Through Indian villages pass troupes of players, enacting the great events of Hindu mythology. The Japanese Noh Play is an elegant survival of a once flourishing union of drama and worship.

By contrast, the Christian Church has often seemed uneasy in its attitude towards the theatre. Perhaps memories still linger of that most hideous of all public performances, the Roman circus, where so many early martyrs met their deaths. More probably the objection is that drama is unpredictable and difficult to control. The theatre can be funny, and some people think it irreverent to laugh in church. It can be all too human, bringing the saints down from their stained-glass windows to appear as living people like ourselves. It can let loose the irresistible forces of the imagination. Taken all in all, the theatre seems likely to be prejudicial to good conduct and ecclesiastical discipline.

In view of this uneasiness, it is curious to note that the central Christian ceremony of the Communion can be seen in one sense as a piece of theatre. The celebrant enacts the role of Christ, repeating in stylised form His words and actions. The others take the part of the Apostles, actually eating and drinking as they did at the Last Supper. Adult audience participation has not been experienced in the modern secular theatre until the last twenty years. When experimental groups began to invite the spectators to take an active part in their plays, the idea was hailed as ingeniously *avant-garde*. The critics did not seem to notice that something very similar had been presented daily in the Christian Church since AD 33.

Much of the ancient ritual that has come down to us is intensely dramatic in form – the processions, the gorgeous costumes, the antiphonal singing and speech, reminiscent of the script of an opera or play. Even today the new bishop knocks with his staff on the west door of the cathedral, and the dean demands to know who is there before he will let him in. Gradually in the late Middle Ages, processions developed into performances, and responses into dialogue. Sober and dignified liturgical drama emerged. It was totally professional – performed exclusively by the priesthood – and was slow to make any concessions to humanity.

The most vivid mediaeval religious drama in England, however, was amateur. Every year at the feast of Corpus Christi, which falls in early summer, the Craft Guilds, or 'Mysteries' as they were called, competed in presenting a dramatised Bible from the Creation of the World to the Last Judgment. They did not perform in the impressive, echoing nave of the cathedral but noisily out in the street. Each 'Mystery' took one scene of the story. In some places, they would perform on decorated booths, while the public milled from one to another like crowds at a funfair. Elsewhere, the stages themselves would trundle round the city, stopping at each square or courtyard to perform their brief scene and then grinding on again. Either way, you could see the whole Cycle performed between breakfast and supper.

Utterly in contrast to liturgical drama, these Mystery Cycles were topical, lusty and even horrifying. Noah has a public row with his wife over getting aboard the Ark; scandalous neighbours giggle lasciviously over Mary's pregnancy; the Crucifixion is presented in hideous detail; the costumes of some of the devils are obscene. This is popular theatre, presented by the local amateurs and mounted regardless of expense.

Some of this liveliness began to feed back into liturgical drama. On Easter morn, the priest and deacon would race down the aisle to the sepulchre as St Peter and St John, with the congregation cheering them on. More and more people began to wonder whether the reverence was not being lost in the fun.

The Reformation drove the theatre out of the church, though a few bands of strolling players managed to keep Christian drama alive into the reign of Elizabeth. In Rufford Old Hall you may see a photocopy of a will, in which the owner left the costumes and properties of his religious touring company to his son, or, if he did not want them, to a young actor called William Shakespeare. Certainly the great flowering of Elizabethan theatre is fed from the soil of religious drama, as you may see clearly enough from *Dr Faustus*, *Measure for Measure* or *The Tempest*. It was left to Oliver Cromwell, in driving the theatre out of respectable life, to destroy its last traces of spirituality.

It is difficult to say which was the greater loser, the Theatre or the Church. For over two hundred years it was difficult to find a single serious play of the highest quality written and acted in the English language, and for much of the eighteenth century the most popular work of Shakespeare was that father of video nasties, *Titus Andronicus*. At the same time, conventional religion in England grew dry and formal, a subject of little interest to the educated man and of dwindling relevance to his humbler neighbour, until great preachers like Wesley suddenly caught the starving public's need for drama. After the endless prosing from the Georgian pulpit, it was almost with relief that the people flocked to hear the Evangelicals threaten them with hellfire.

Of all people, the man who brought religion back into the theatre was Ibsen, who was promptly reviled by half the clergy in England. He scandalised late Victorian society, not only by trespassing on the Church's territory but by his extraordinary stand on questions like respectability and women's rights. To many he seemed to be Antichrist, but he raised drama to its old position as one of the greatest of the arts by restoring its spirituality. Many of his plays are charged with religious overtones, and his two poetic masterpieces, *Brandt* and *Peer Gynt*, dared to speak of God and humankind with a shocking honesty undreamt of for centuries.

At the same time cultivated Europe became aware of an extraordinary Passion Play performed every ten years at a Bavarian village called Oberammergau ever since 1663 in thankfulness for its miraculous escape from the Plague. On the London stage *The Miracle* managed to creep past the Lord Chamberlain by the device of having no words for him to censor. Rather more subtly, a modern morality play with a mysterious angelic figure was set in a boarding-house and enjoyed a long run as

The Passing of the Third Floor Back. In 1920 Joan of Arc was canonised, and three years later George Bernard Shaw, England's greatest disciple of Ibsen, wrote a great masterpiece in her honour, mainly in order to prevent its being written by a churchgoer.

In 1928 the Theatre moved back into the Church, when Masefield's *Coming of Christ* was presented at Canterbury, the first dramatic performance to be shown in an English cathedral since the Reformation. This was the beginning of the Canterbury Festival, from which, in 1935, T. S. Eliot's *Murder in the Cathedral* transferred to the West End and Broadway, triumphantly carrying the Church back into the Theatre. During the Second World War, E. Martin Browne toured the country with the Pilgrim Players, the very first theatrical company ever to receive financial support from the British Government. At the same time the BBC presented a modern dramatised life of Christ by Dorothy L. Sayers called *A Man Born to be King*.

Where the professionals led, the amateur movement was quick to follow. In 1929 the Religious Drama Society of Great Britain was founded to provide scripts, advice and training for church drama groups. In 1931 Bishop Bell appointed a Diocesan Drama Adviser for Chichester, and soon other dioceses followed suit. One by one, the other churches began to admit the value of drama; to encourage or even sponsor Christian plays, revues and musicals. Today there are thousands of such performances in Britain every year, given by Anglicans, Roman Catholics, Methodists, United Reformed, Baptists, Quakers and many others.

Now that the revival has come, we should perhaps learn some lessons from what went wrong last time. Drama, like all the other arts, has something of immense value to offer to religion, and both tend to wither if they are separated. But they will only thrive together as partners, not as master and slave. It must be recognised that the playwright, as much as the preacher, speaks with the voice of genuine inspiration. You cannot determine whether a play is truly religious by the test of pious conformism, for the theatre loses its most precious gift of spontaneity if it is too severely disciplined. Dignity and reverence are real virtues, but they are not the same as pompous servility. Nor, as too much of the Communist theatre shows us, is truth always to be found by walking along the party line to the bitter end. Do not ask what is the message; messages are for commercials, not for real drama. Ask instead, 'Does this play give life and give it more abundantly?'

Religious Drama
what is it for?

Music has long been accepted as a vital ingredient of worship. Hymns, psalms set to music, plain-chant, organ voluntaries, choirs and solo singers form an integral part of most church services. Many of us would find worship pedantic and dry without music, which colours our liturgy and adds a fresh dimension to the spoken word in prayers and sermons.

Also, over the years, visual art has possessed an accepted place in our churches. Stained-glass windows told Bible stories to those who were not able to read; pictures of saints reminded people of the great Christians who had preceded them; tombs were often topped by works of art in marble and stone; choir stalls were decorated with patterns of leaves and flowers; arches and pillars came alive with the carved figures of artisans, kings and queens, animals and birds. Many modern churches use stained glass, carved wood and stone, tapestry and painting to remind congregations of various aspects of their faith. Architects use their imaginative skill to create buildings whose spires, domes, star-shapes or cubes signify a spirit of worship.

And then there is poetry – an accepted art form which has resulted in the accumulation of hundreds of hymns and songs and found ex-pression in prayers and in translations of the Scriptures.

Music, visual arts, poetry – they are all an accepted part of our Christian heritage, and yet what has happened to drama? Why has it become the poor relation of the other arts? Perhaps the oldest of them all in terms of worship, drama was expelled during the puritan revolution and has only begun to creep back into churches during this century.

Why has there been such a prejudice against drama in churches? Perhaps the answer lies in its very personal nature. Music, sculpture, painting, architecture and poetry are not quite so immediate in their effect as a play which involves living people acting and reacting on one another. Drama cannot help being immediate. It is a 'happening', a piece of life being lived before our eyes. We find ourselves involved in the situations of a play almost as much as in the quarrels, arguments and crossing of emotions that go on in our own homes. There is no escape from the demands the play makes on us. We are drawn into this orbit of human beings caught up in resolution and irresolution and, for the time being, our own problems become shelved in consideration of the problems on stage.

Perhaps it is this immediacy of drama which prompted Jesus to teach by way of parable. Of course we remember his precepts, but it is the parables which really stick in our memory and go on working inside us, relating this parable to that part of our life, whether it be the Good Samaritan, the woman with the pieces of silver, the Wedding Feast, or the Prodigal Son.

Most of the parables are not tied up at the end with neat explanations, and so we find them niggling at our consciences to be resolved in our own behaviour. There is no 'thou shalt not' about the parables and yet how much are we all warned against becoming like the priest and the Levite in the Good Samaritan; the elder brother in the Prodigal Son; the man with the single talent; rich Dives ignoring the beggar at his gate; or the lazy, uncaring foolish Virgins?

Drama is about the immediacy of human living. It continually reminds us that we are not alone, that we should never be isolating ourselves in an ivory tower of subjective holiness, that we have been commanded to care for our neighbours. And for this reason drama frightens us. We prefer not to be reminded of our shortcomings as human beings; to come out from church bathed in a golden glow of holiness rather than to see ourselves under the searchlight of truth.

Drama can remind us that our religion is not like some trains, 'For Sundays only', but is a living, difficult and daily struggle to come to terms with our own shortcomings and with the tiresomenesses of other people. Drama is very much about the relationships we have with our neighbours. And for that reason it is heady stuff and we are possibly right to be scared of it.

So, if someone says to you, 'What is the point of your putting on a play at St Mary's?' you can begin by assuring them that a play has the power to teach, like the parables of Jesus, and, in that sense, has a rightful place in the church. If they argue that the idea of drama is out of tradition with the church, you can remind them that the very first drama in this country sprang from the early church liturgies. And you can also remark that the other arts, music, painting, sculpture, architecture and poetry have been and are included in forms of worship in most Christian churches, in one aspect or another.

Drama can also be a means for inviting those who are not worshipping Christians to your church. Most of us are diffident (and rightly so) about twisting people's arms to go with us to worship. But it is quite another matter to invite friends to a play in the church. We live in a secular age where so many have the oddest notions about churches. 'I'm too happy to be a Christian' was said by a woman who had never actually attended a church service in her life. 'Churches are such miserable places!' is the fairly constant cry among those ignorant of any experience of going to a service. It's not easy to persuade people that most Christians are warm, kindly, happy folk, or that our services are occasions for praise and joy. The play in church provides an ideal way for inviting strangers inside our churches. Quite a number of those who go to a church for the first time to see a play, go back afterwards to attend services.

And then there is the opportunity for ecumenism. If your drama group is made up of varying brands of Christians, the play will draw you all together in a new way. What's more, you will find yourselves sharing your special insights regarding faith, in relation to the play. Catholics, Baptists, Friends, Methodists, United Reformed Churchpeople, Anglicans, working together can learn so much from one another, and of course the production should prove all the richer for such diversity.

Drama, too, can bring out gifts in quite unexpected people. The little 'mouse' who sits at the back of a side aisle each Sunday may suddenly blossom when given a character to play. You may discover that a morose sidesman who frowns over the offertory has a surprising gift for comedy; that the worried little Sunday School teacher can dance; or that the particularly naughty boy in the choir plays the part of a young Joseph with a startling sincerity.

Drama demands a release of emotion which can have beneficial effects on the participants. A young woman who had married in her teens and found herself, in her late twenties, resenting her role of mother to two children to the extent that she was contemplating suicide, found her life straightening out and gathering meaning after she had been persuaded to join a local church drama group. Emotions that might have wrecked her marriage were released for her in a striking performance of Mary Magdalene.

Drama is a mission to the heart. A young man, desperate and lonely, having lost his mother and without a job or faith, came to see a performance of *The Pilgrim's Progress* by John Bunyan. The character of Christian attracted his attention from the moment the play began. He identified with Christian's falling into the Slough of Despond and with his imprisonment in Doubting Castle by Giant Despair. Then, as the play proceeded, he began to identify with Christian's increasing hopefulness and trust in God till, by the time the play ended, he knew that he wanted to become a Christian. We met him some years later, radiantly happy, in work, and with a wife who seemed as delighted with life as he was.

Religious drama can certainly change lives. But beware of the play which preaches. Jesus scarcely ever provided neat ends to his parables. Let the play tell the story with all its undercurrents of human joys and sorrows, failings and triumphs, betrayals and faiths, and let the audience go away to work out the 'message' for themselves. There is never any one 'message'. Even in the parables we probably all take away different meanings according to our needs. So in the play, let it be true to human nature and the audience will draw from it just what each individual needs at that moment.

Choose your play, then, primarily for its truth about people and for its understanding of, and love for them. Avoid at all costs those plays which form glib judgements – when we know from the start that Mr and Mrs Good are going to end up in a comfortable home with well-behaved children while Mr and Mrs Bad will die horrid deaths in a road accident. Such plays are all too common, and possibly do more harm than good to the very cause they are trying to serve. There is something specious about the idea of 'Be good and you will prosper'. Too many of the world's saints teach us by their lives of suffering that being converted is no easy matter. We need to beware of selling Christianity cheap.

If your play is to be based on a Biblical theme, the characters will suddenly spring alive from the pages of history to become human beings with problems and hopes and trusts very much the same as our own. 'So, it was all in the past!' becomes changed to 'It might be happening today!' Children and young people, especially, can learn the relevance of Bible stories by acting them. Those of us who know the stories so well that we tend to stop listening to them find them suddenly absorbing and challenging. It's as if the flat pictures in one's mind leaped into three-dimensional reality like the cut-out pop-up pictures in childrens' books. Moses, Abraham, Joseph, David, Ruth, the Apostles, Mary, Mary Magdalene, Herod, Pilate, and Jesus himself, become real people with faces and arms and legs; working, talking, sleeping, eating, praying, suffering like the rest of us.

Some of the most powerful religious plays presented in churches are modern and present challenges to our consciences on many levels. 'I didn't come to a play in church to be made uncomfortable!', an elderly lady complained to the vicar after one of Theatre Roundabout's shows, 'I come to church to be comforted.' The vicar preached on that subject the following Sunday.

How many of us 'come to church to be comforted'? How many of us like to use our faith as a kind of eiderdown or duvet to protect us from the chill dark night of our doubts and fears?

True drama can serve as a living sermon to strip away, as that vicar did, the notion that faith is a cosy panacea for all ills. True drama, whether Biblical or contemporary, whether about the life of a saint or ordinary everyday people, should strip off coverings of sentimentality, of intolerance, of judgementalism, of easy answers – to reveal the hard, bare bones of truth and the fiery pain of love.

True religious drama should not be afraid to laugh at the religious, to critise the pious or to challenge the preconceptions of the hidebound.

Drama in church can be seen as an awakener of conscience as much for the audience as for the performers. If it is fun to do, so much the better. If it is funny, better still; nothing stirs our consciences so well as a good joke.

In this way we can see drama in our churches as an enhancement of worship, and not an optional 'extra' tagged on at the end of the curriculum. Drama had its very roots in the church. Without the Christian Church there might be no National Theatre today. In divorcing drama from church worship we run the danger of worship becoming too remote, too cerebral; and in doing so we find, to our dismay, that our emotional lives have remained outside the reach of the Church.

Perhaps drama is one of the means by which we can most readily run back into her arms?

THREE

Starting a drama group in your church

Let us suppose that you are an enthusiast for Religious Drama; maybe you are a member of the clergy, a teacher, an amateur actor with some particular knowledge of the subject; perhaps you have had no experience at all but feel instinctively that Religious Drama is of immense potential value; but how do you begin?

First of all you will need to fire three or four others with your own enthusiasm and hope that they will each encourage at least one other friend to think in terms of forming a group. If you succeed here you will have a nucleus of about eight or nine people, which is all you will need to begin with.

But do move with caution. Unless you have begun with nine people as enthusiastic as you are yourself, you will have to go gently if you are not going to scare them off. Most people have an ambivalent feeling about acting which at once fascinates and scares them. You will want to work on their fascination and try not to scare them during the first, formative weeks of your group's life.

Possibly the ideal way to begin is to embark on a series of play-readings. You can ring the changes of venue so that people take it in turn to play 'host'. At this stage you will need time to get to know one another, so don't make these readings too formal. Make sure that there will be an interval for coffee and biscuits.Or you may suggest that those taking part bring sandwiches with them and have time to chat together before the reading begins. The friendly atmosphere will do much to take away the scared feeling of the shy members of your group and gradually they will gain confidence.

How should you set about casting these plays? To start with you may know very little about the capabilities of your group and everything will have to be achieved by trial and error. At this stage it's best for one person to act as the leader of the group for any given reading. This role can vary from person to person, but it's essential to have one leader per reading, unless you are going to end up with arguments and frustrations. Your casting will have to be arbitrary for your initial readings; but very soon it will become apparent who is best at reading what, and the task will become easier.

Then comes the actual choice of your play. Who makes it? Here again it's best to take this in turn. If A chose the play last week, let B choose it next week, or next month, or whenever you plan to meet. Of course it wouldn't be very satisfactory to read a play which only A or B likes. There must be some consensus of agreement as to what play should be read. Try to vary the type of play as much as possible. Ring the changes between poetry and prose, comedy and tragedy, ancient and modern. It will give everyone a chance to show what their range of talent is and it will make you all acquainted with many different types of plays.

After you have been reading for some time, you may feel brave enough to invite a small audience to listen to you. If you do this you will need at least one rehearsal beforehand. Here again the leader of your group (or leader for that one week or month) should be the one to take the rehearsal, to cast the play and to make any changes he or she thinks necessary.

Of course the moment your readers are confronted by an audience they will be scared all over again. By this time you will have gained enough of their confidence to tell them that acting *is* a scary business and that they will never escape that sense of 'butterflies in the stomach' when performing, and that the only way to cope lies in the work of preparation. Persuade all your readers to work on their parts so that they can be read easily and fluently. The 'butterflies' won't go, but at least they can be quietened.

There will be an added satisfaction in reading to an audience. For the first time your group will have a sense of sharing what they are doing, sharing their delight in the play and their faith in what it has to say. And they will begin to discover some kind of audience reaction. Did they laugh at the bits you all thought so funny? Did they fidget during the most dramatic moments? You will learn a lot from the way in which your audience responds.

There is a tendency among actors to be interested only in the scenes in which they appear, and to be less involved with the play as a whole. But in a reading everyone is a sitting duck and so everyone becomes involved with the play. This helps a lot with the cultivation of atmosphere. The more any actor has become involved with the whole, the more he will seem to be grounded in the scenes in which he takes part. Ultimately it is the play which your group will be presenting to the audience, not a series of scenes which give opportunities for individuals to shine.

A word of caution to the 'leaders' who will be responsible for casting. In your search for ability and talent you will be giving the shy ones as much encouragement as you can; but you will also be presented with the problem of those who are inclined to be over-confident. You may meet one or two who feel they should have leading parts on the strength of having played a lead once when they were at school. A great deal of tact needs to be exercised during this period of discovering talents, and the 'leader's' decision must be final. But do ring the changes as much as possible with your readers, as well as with your choice of plays. Give everyone a chance to play large as well as small parts and vary your casting even though it may involve people reading roles for which they might appear unsuited. A lot of mistakes will be made, but you will get a lot of surprises!

After you have been going for several months, you may feel brave enough to introduce the idea of holding workshops. It could be that one of your 'leaders' will have had enough experience in this field to be able to take the sessions. If not, you may want to call in the help of an expert. Possibly a local drama adviser or teacher of drama could be prevailed upon to help you.

You will have reached the stage when your group should be weaned from the security of a chair and a book to take part in exercises which will make them feel vulnerable. Naturally, the play readings will have done a lot to break down inhibitive shyness and embarrassment. Now you will be going one stage further and asking them to make fools of themselves. Because that's what such workshops are about and for that reason it's a good idea to think of them as 'theatre games'. Don't, whatever you do, allow these to be taken seriously. Bring a party spirit to the event, allow for a lot of giggling, and everyone will enjoy them-selves, quite forgetting the main purpose of what they are doing, which is to limber up. Don't make the games too difficult at first. They are to be enjoyed rather than endured. Choose simple ones like passing on a joke – one person miming the telling of something funny to his or her neighbour followed by the neighbour laughing and passing it on to the next person, till, finally, you get a complete circle all laughing. You can play a similar game with miming the bringing of bad news.

You can have fun by turning the group into animals from Noah's Ark. The 'leader' puts names of animals into a hat and each member draws a name and mimes the animal while the rest guess what the animal is. Try miming different kinds of movement – running up and down stairs, skating, kicking a ball, riding a bicycle. You can graduate from such light-hearted exercises to the more serious matter of miming human characters. Suggest that everyone, in turn, should walk across the room as very old, very young, lame, distressed, excited, despairing. All these will involve the use of feeling as well as that of body movement.

Gradually you will have given everyone an opportunity to loosen up, to be a bit of a clown, to use their bodies and their imaginations and to express emotion.

Dancing is a great loosener of limbs and you might end your session by putting on the radio or a tape recorder and letting your group move to the music. Some of them may complain that they 'look like Charlies' – but explain to them that all acting is about looking 'like a Charlie' – and that if they jib at that they had better pack it in and take up Bridge instead. There is an element of the clown in all acting without which a curious divide opens up between actor and audience. If the actor is thinking, 'I hope I'm not making a fool of myself', he is instantly distancing himself from those who are watching him. He will be putting up a smug little fence around his personality which will indicate 'thus far and no farther'. If on the other hand the actor can forget himself sufficiently to be as much of a 'Charlie' as his role demands, the audience will love him for his openness, will feel with his predicaments and share in his laughter.

By this time certain members of your group may be clamouring to put on a play. So what are you to do? Are you going to put on a full-length play, possibly one of the ones you have been reading? Or does the prospect of a long play seem a little daunting? There's a lot to be said for producing something simpler for a start. So far you have been reading a variety of plays and have limbered yourselves up with the theatre games and some of the more serious mimes. But are you quite ready to face a play with two, or possibly three, acts?

At this stage in the development of your group you might consider beginning your plunge into real drama with something which could be called 'drama in worship'. This is a piece of theatre which can be slotted into a church service. It will have the advantage of being short, and you will have a ready-made audience.

But will you all be quite confident enough to face performing to so many of those people in the pews who will be known to you? It was one thing to read plays aloud to them, but quite another to get up and act in front of them, however short the piece may be.

Would it be so scaring to perform to total strangers in the street? If the answer is 'no', then what about beginning your debut with some street theatre? Street plays usually last only about three or four minutes. Their effects have to be broad ones otherwise nobody will stop to look and listen. You will need to wear exaggerated costumes to attract attention and above all you will be forced to speak up if your voices are not to be lost in the roar of traffic or the noise of shopping crowds in a precinct. (Don't forget to ask permission from the police first.)

Advice on short scripts of all kinds can be found in the RADIUS

Library (Religious Drama Society of GB). You may want to make up your own short plays, or act scenes from Scripture. This is not quite so daunting as it would seem. Passers-by are usually extremely friendly and good-humoured. Of course some of them will resent your appearance on 'their' pavement and will walk straight through your scene to establish their right of way. But these will be exceptions. Most people welcome any diversion in the High Street and will stay to watch for a few minutes. Bring two or three very short plays with you and you may find some of your audience staying till the end. This will test your ability to hold attention and you will learn a lot about what will, and will not, engage people.

Above all, you will have broken the ice and will have gained confidence.

Another possibility for your first plunge is taking a short piece of drama into a hospital. You will be warmly welcomed. But don't expect the same kind of reaction that the shoppers will give you. Sick people are tired and often in pain and will not have the energy to respond enthusiastically. But they will be grateful for a break from the radio and compulsory television. The same is even more true in old peoples' homes. They will be pleased to have you; but because their minds may not be as bright as they once were, and because of failing sight and hearing, their reactions to you may prove disappointing. This doesn't mean that such audiences won't teach you a lot about what you are doing and your work may be of more ultimate value in such places than anywhere you could choose to perform. And remember that acting improves with acting. There is no short cut to acquiring self-confidence and ability.

By this time your group will be growing in that self-confidence and may feel ready to act in front of 'all those people they know so well' in the church. The group will have developed the assurance of becoming an entity. There will be a spirit of teamwork among everyone, a sense of belonging to each other. This is splendid, and to be welcomed. But beware of the danger of growing inwards. It's all too easy to become so absorbed in the process of making a play that the outside world seems to become irrelevant. Don't, as a group, stop being interested in the news, in the world of the arts, in sport, in philosophy and, above all, in the people around you. As an actor you can find your abilities stretched and enhanced by your interest in the world outside.

Don't become ingrowing and isolated. Go to other groups' productions whenever you get an opportunity, whether amateur or professional. There is always so much to learn from watching other actors. The 'leaders' or if they may have become by now, directors, will learn much from watching the work of other directors. So don't arrange your rehearsals on a night when some visiting company may be performing in your area. Go to see that company, if possible, as a group. Make a point of getting to professional theatre, as a group, at least three or four times a year. Watching plays with your new insights as actors or directors will deepen your appreciation of them and teach you more than you could imagine.

So now you are ready to perform in church.

What will you decide to do?

Will it be a full-length play? Will it be something that can fit unobtrusively into a service? Will you do something that could involve the congregation?

The next two chapters are intended to help you make that decision.

Drama in worship

One of the simplest ways in which to introduce your church to drama is to put a piece of theatre into the context of a service. By its very nature it will be short and its theme should be relevant to the theme of the worship for that day. Besides, a congregation which has become acclimatised to such brief moments of drama will be more ready to accept a full-length play at a later date.

There are many ways of introducing drama into a church service and one of the least complicated is for a newly-formed drama group to arrange for the dramatised reading of some piece of Scripture. Many Biblical stories and scenes spring to life more sharply when the characters are dramatised. Your group might like to involve the congregation as well. There are quite a number of crowd scenes in the Bible and these can be effective when read by a large body of people.

Think of the moment when a rather shy individual has been asked to read the Lesson For The Day and words get mumbled and stumbled over. The temptation for the average churchgoer is to feel, 'Oh well, I know that anyway', and to switch off. But imagine taking the same passage, breaking it up into the speaking characters and the narrative, and reading it like that. Immediately everyone in the church becomes involved and what had seemed too familiar to be arresting, suddenly leaps into focus.

For example: from *8:41-56 St Luke*

JAIRUS: And, behold, there came a man named Jairus, and he was a ruler of the synagogue; and he fell down at Jesus' feet, and besought him that he would come into his house. For he had one only daughter, about twelve years of age, and she lay a dying.

CROWD: But as he went the people thronged him.

WOMAN: And a woman having an issue of blood twelve years, which had spent all her living upon physicians, neither could be healed of any, came behind him, and touched the borders of his garment:

NARRATOR: and immediately her issue of blood stanched.

JESUS: And Jesus said, Who touched me?

CROWD: When all denied,

PETER: Peter, and they that were with him said, Master, the multitude throng thee and press thee, and sayest thou, Who touched me?

JESUS: And Jesus said, Somebody hath touched me: for I perceive that virtue is gone out of me.

WOMAN: And when the woman saw that she was not hid, she came trembling, and falling down before him, she declared unto him before all the people for what cause she had touched him, and how she was healed immediately.

JESUS: And he said unto her, Daughter be of good comfort: thy faith hath made thee whole: go in peace.

NARRATOR: While he yet spake, there cometh one from the ruler of the synagogue's house, saying to him,

SERVANT: Thy daughter is dead; trouble not the Master.

JESUS: But when Jesus heard it he answered him, saying, Fear not: believe only, and she shall be made whole.

NARRATOR: And when he came into the house, he suffered no man to go in,

PETER: save Peter,

JAMES: and James,

JOHN: and John

NARRATOR: and the father and the mother of the maiden.

CROWD: And all wept and bewailed her:

JESUS: but he said, Weep not: she is not dead, but sleepeth.

CROWD: And they laughed him to scorn, knowing that she was dead.

NARRATOR: And he put them all out, and took her by the hand, and called, saying,

JESUS: Maid, arise.

DAUGHTER: And her spirit came again, and she arose straightway:

JESUS: and he commanded to give her meat.

NARRATOR: And her parents were astonished;

JESUS: but he charged them that they should tell no man what was done.

By dividing the story like this, the life in it is released and something of its original impact is restored. Because the story *is* an amazing one. It is intensely dramatic. The incident of the bleeding woman becomes a sub plot to the main drama of Jairus and his dying child. We become aware of those crowds pressing in on Jesus, of the woman frightened to touch him and yet clinging to his garment, of the disciples almost making a joke when he asks, 'Who touched me?' And one wonder leads on to another. We hear that the child is dead and everyone expects the story to be over. But Jesus turns everyone's expectations upside down, so astonishingly so, that the crowd laughs at him.

At this moment the story begins to touch our own lives. Had we been in that crowd of mourners would we have laughed, too? Have there not been many moments in our own lives when we have thought, 'The child is dead, trouble not the Master.' Suddenly we become aware of the link between the story and ourselves – that link which is an essential ingredient of all great drama.

We perceive that the story is not a beautiful legend told poetically which has little to do with real life, but an account of real people leading practical, everyday lives, just like ourselves, to whom marvellous things have happened.

Even such a brief reading needs preparation and your characters and narrator will have spent two or three evenings in rehearsal. You can't, of course, expect the congregation to rehearse with you. In any case this would take away some of the impact of the drama. So you will have to let them have duplicated sheets with their lines marked clearly. It might be helpful to have your leader or director among them to give them a lead.

During your rehearsals try to hold at least one of them in the church itself. You will be surprised how difficult church acoustics can be, and for this reason let everyone involved in the reading take it in turns to listen to the others from the back of the building. It will be a different matter from reading in a room or playing theatre games.

Such readings can be given by ordinary members of a congregation who may have no connection with any recognised drama group. In this case the minister or priest in charge of the church would possibly be the best person to rehearse the readers. Dramatised readings provide an opportunity to involve those who wouldn't dare to take part in anything as ambitious as a short sketch, a mime, an anthology, or a voice drama.

Buf if we are thinking now of the drama group who *are* feeling their way towards something more ambitious, let us consider the possibilities of these other alternatives.

It's easy to know where Scripture readings fit in with a morning or evening service, but where do we put the short sketch? Anything you do will, of course, be arranged in consultation with the clergy in charge who may have a variety of suggestions to make. The most obvious place for the short sketch is for it to take the place of the sermon; in which case the sketch should reflect the theme of the service. Don't feel that it has to be deadly serious. Most sermons have jokes in them, so don't be frightened of using a comedy theme. Be sure not to make it too long. Six or seven minutes is the outside. Make sure that it is well rehearsed and that you have a director for this who will plan the moves.

Then comes the question of being seen. Many churches have excellent raised areas which can be used. If not, do get hold of a platform. Your comedy will fall flat if people can't see your faces. You won't need stage lighting for something which should look as natural as possible in the context of a service, though you must have *some* light on your faces or the impact will be lost.

What will you choose to put on? There are quite a number of sketches published such as *Time to Act* by Riding Lights. Or you might think of writing your own. *Don't* make it too long, and *do* make it relevant. *Don't* make it funny at the expense of being snide. And *do* make sure that it has something positive to say. Your sketch may be taking the place of the sermon. You don't want people to wish they had been given a sermon instead.

Mime can be used effectively in conjunction with the reading of Scripture, particularly when it is telling a story. Here it's simplest to have only one reader and allow the mime to colour the story. For this you might like to think in terms of using as much of the church as possible – the aisles as well as the chancel and possibly the pulpit. A mime is ideal for presenting a crowd scene. Imagine miming the story of Jairus' daughter. You could have the crowd pressing up the aisle; the house could be the chancel and you might even make the pulpit into the room where the little girl is sleeping. This might be an ideal opportunity for a youth group. Those nervous of learning lines find it less exacting to memorise movement. But this doesn't mean that the mime should not be carefully rehearsed. Each movement should be planned by the director who will probably call a number of rehearsals. Ask your reader to be present at all later rehearsals. He or she should become as familiar with the detailed movement in the mime as the mime group with the exact words of the reading. Once again, this will be a means by which the words of Scripture can be made to come alive and become exciting and immediate; and the effect will be felt no less by the congregation than by the performers themselves.

A short anthology can often be given a significant place in a church service. Here you can take a little longer, say, up to ten or twelve minutes. You will be making a mosaic of pieces - poems, prose, stories, possibly something from a play, even scraps from a newspaper - around a theme. It will give a number of people a chance to take part and to use different styles of acting. You will need a good director for this and the keynote will be variety. The anthology show is not as easy as it looks. Your group should take time to find the right pieces and be ready to discard those which do not fit in. The theme should move in thought from one item to the next. Suppose your subject to be Christmas. You take a passage from Dickens, put it next to *The Journey of the Magi* by T. S. Eliot, include a scene from *Christmas in the Market-Place* by Henri Ghéon and end up with Eleanor Farjeon's *Carol of the Signs*. They are all about Christmas. True. But there is no continuity. Your anthology has not taken you anywhere. But if you had begun with *The Carol of the Signs* and taken the theme of all those who had made their way to Bethlehem on Christmas night, finally relating this to our own journey to the Holy Child – you would have intrigued your audience and set them thinking.

Had you thought of presenting a voice drama? (An example of one of these is given in the Appendix at the end of this book.) Between half a dozen and twenty people make an ideal number for a kind of drama which is mainly vocal.

The idea is to use both choral and solo speaking and to make this use as varied as possible. Such pieces can be put almost anywhere in a service, depending on their theme. Suppose your group consists of ten, four men and six women. You can produce a great number of vocal variations such as: the four men speaking, the six women speaking, two men and two women, one man and three women, five women and two men – and so on. And then you can build up from one or two voices gradually till you have everyone speaking in a grand crescendo. And there will be the telling moments when a solo voice speaks. In every case the tone and tempo can be varied to colour the words.

The example at the end of this book might give you ideas about creating such a voice drama yourself. The technique isn't limited to any particular style. Try experimenting with poetry. What about using passages from great works such as *The Pilgrim's Progress*, *The Great Divorce*, *Murder in the Cathedral* as well as the Bible itself. Like the sketch, the mime and the anthology, voice dramas should be related to the theme of the service and should fit naturally and unobtrusively into the pattern of your worship, so that it doesn't look like a piece of blue cloth patched on to a red garment.

And like the others you will need a great deal of careful rehearsal. Preferably choose a director who has some experience in the use of voice or reading poetry.

What do you do about movement in a voice drama? Ideally there should be a limited amount of mobility to give the impression of a living group. But the movement is best kept to the group and should not break away from it. Think of the group in terms of a picture rather than putting them in rows like people posing for a photograph. Let them use limited movements such as the turning of the head, the occasional use of hand or arm gesture, the twist of the body, the body raised on tiptoe or dropped onto knees. No one should stand out from the others by breaking from the picture. The group represents the voice of humanity and we in the congregation will find ourselves identifying with that voice.

There are one or two practical points to be considered for all these forms of using drama in worship. The first is what do we wear? Although the sketch will demand its own costumes, the other types of drama call for some kind of unifying dress. Don't mix too many styles, particularly in the readings and the voice dramas. It's a bit jarring to see lounge suits worn next to jeans, coats and skirts jostling with long Indian dresses. Some sort of overall simple effect will take the minds of the congregation off your individual appearance and keep them concentrating on what you have to say. In this way your group will be seen to be organic.

By this time you will probably have thought of other ways in which drama may be introduced into worship, possibly using dance, song, or instrumental music as ingredients. There are so many ways in which to achieve that heightening and revitalising of our church services brought about by the use of drama, and you will need to find just the right one for your group.

Show careful consideration to the feelings and prejudices of the congregation. Remember they may find what you do upsetting and startling. Work closely and prayerfully with the clergy and above all, rehearse, rehearse, rehearse . . . till the meaning of what you are doing shines out with clarity.

Launching out on a play

Sooner or later the time is going to come when you will want to present a real play. With any luck, your group will be longing to get their teeth into one, but, if not, be cautious how you push them. The success of any dramatic production is directly related to the personal commitment of every single person involved, so talking people into a play they don't really want to do is usually a recipe for failure.

People who have seen your sketches or drama in worship may also suggest that you should put on something more ambitious. This too is important. For a play you will not have a captive congregation for audience; you will need to persuade people to make a special journey to church, and that is not so easy as you might think. On winter nights the building may be notoriously chilly, on the long summer evenings the garden beckons invitingly, and all the year round you have a doughty competitor in the television set. As well as a production team, you will also need an audience.

Finally, you must feel really confident of the church authorities. The most important, of course, are the clergy. If they are behind you, heart and soul, they can tip the balance between success and failure, particularly in persuading people to come to the show. Get your clergy interested from the beginning. Discuss the whole project with them, consult them over the choice of play, invite them to rehearsals, make them feel that it is *their* show in their church, and then they will do their utmost to help you. Otherwise you may find your play relegated to the boring tail of church notices: 'I have been asked to announce . . .'

The clergy are not the only powers you will need to consider. The organist and choirmaster/mistress can be very important to you, either as an obstacle or an ally. You will not be very popular if you want to rehearse in the church on choir practice night, and it is almost impossible to think, let alone do anything creative, while one of the organist's pupils is trying to master Bach's Toccata and Fugue in B Minor.

All the other church officials are likely to be affected in some way or another by your production, most of all the long-suffering verger or caretaker, who is apt to feel rather like a tired mother who has to watch her beloved house trampled through by her children's ghastly friends. You may want to ask the church council for financial help, and other church members might be kind enough to do refreshments. Remember that all these people may feel that the church is *their* church and that you are in danger of trespassing on their territory.

Before embarking on any irreversible step, take everyone concerned into your confidence, listen to their advice, explain your problems and assess their willingness to help. With their backing your task will be a hundred times easier, and, even if some remain unenthusiastic, you may be able to ensure their benevolent neutrality.

Now that you have an enthusiastic cast, an interested public and co-operative church authorities, your first need will be to find a suitable script.

Where on earth do we look?

There are surprisingly few play publishers in Britain, and only a tiny proportion of their output could possibly be described as religious. If you are lucky enough to have a local bookshop with a section on drama, do go and browse among the paperbacks, but you are unlikely to find what you want, and if you ask the assistants if any of their plays are religious, you will get some startled looks.

Those are nothing, however, to the looks you may get if you go into a religious bookshop and ask for plays. The chances are that the only ones will be found in the children's section, and they may prove unbearably naïve. It is true that at this stage you should be looking for something simple, but do not snatch at a script that will insult the intelligence of your cast and audience simply because it is the first thing to hand.

You may have better luck visiting your public library, especially if it is a large one or belongs to a circulating group. They may even have a special drama catalogue, set out like publishers' lists, giving the length of the play, number of men and women in the cast and possibly a synopsis of the story. Some libraries actually lend complete sets of plays (one for each performer plus one each for the director and stage manager) which you can borrow for the period of rehearsal. If you do, then treat them lovingly, and never mark the scripts with anything but pencil. In any case, a sympathetic librarian can be a wonderful adviser.

Of course you can write to the publishers themselves. Samuel French, for instance, publish a periodical catalogue called *Play Parade*. Most of the items are recent West End successes and unlikely to be of much use to you, but they do have special sections devoted to religious drama and one-act plays. The other leading play publishers are Methuen, Faber and Penguin. Their authors tend to be more 'interesting', and they seem to select on the principle that the play must be worth reading as well as seeing. There are also a number of smaller publishers who specialise in scripts for amateurs. Their advertisements appear regularly in the magazine, *Amateur Stage*.

The British Theatre Association (once called the British Drama League) is the largest and best-equipped of the various societies that exist to help amateurs. They are not of course particularly concerned with religious work, and the specialists for your immediate purpose are undoubtedly RADIUS, which is an acronym for the Religious Drama Society of Great Britain. They run a large lending library of Christian playscripts and can lend individual copies or complete sets. Their librarians are voluntary and do not work full-time, but they are most helpful and have unrivalled experience of advising church drama groups.

Unlike the public libraries, RADIUS and the British Theatre Association are not free. Their services are available only to members, but their subscriptions are modest, and, once you have joined, there is very little further expense. They will send you classified, descriptive play lists, let you have sample copies to read before hiring a set, and advise you if you are still in doubt.

How are we to choose out of all these?
None of these sources will be of much use to you unless you have a fairly clear idea of what you want to do, and the first step is to rule out the impossible. Before making any plans you must take stock of your resources and face up to your limitations.

Your most valuable assets are your potential performers, so think about them first. How many men and women are available to appear in your play, and what are their abilities? If you only have a small number, you can forget plays with large casts, and it would be silly to attempt a musical if nobody can sing or dance. If your group are predominantly women, or men, or young, or old, you will have to reject a lot of unsuitable scripts.

The same applies to scenery, furniture and other material effects. If you haven't got them or can't use them, that narrows the choice still further. Costumes are another important point. They are expensive to hire, difficult and laborious to make. Can you provide them, or must you stick to a play which can be performed in ordinary modern dress?

As you can see, the list of possibilities is dwindling. The best thing about not having much at your disposal is that a lot of decisions are taken for you by circumstances.

For your comfort, a number of authors have recognised your problems in advance, and there are quite a number of small-cast modern-dress religious plays available which are within the compass of the most limited drama group. If you are all men or (more probably) all women, there are plays written for you, and there are a substantial number intended especially for children.

The final limitation you have to consider is the building in which you are to present this play. You may, of course, opt for the church hall, where you can hope to find some of the conventional theatrical advantages, such as a stage and perhaps even some lighting, but even there you are likely to encounter serious shortcomings. Moreover, many churches are beautiful places, charged with atmosphere and a sense of the presence of God, whereas most church halls are not. If you decide to use the church, you will almost certainly run into practical difficulties, but your surroundings will offer many compensations, not least because of their subtle effect on the audience.

The problems of playing in church will be discussed in detail at a later stage of this book, but they will all have to be considered before you make a final choice of play. If all these material considerations, all this worldly wisdom, sound a little lacking in faith, let us remember the words of Our Lord Himself, as they appear in St Luke, Chapter 14, verses 28–30 (NIV). 'Suppose one of you wants to build a tower. Will he not first sit down and estimate the cost to see if he has enough money to complete it? For if he lays the foundation and is not able to finish it, everyone who sees it will ridicule him, saying, "This fellow began to build and was not able to finish".' Your play is the tower that you are going to build to the finish.

So far we have only looked at the difficulties, but every bit as important is the intention of the production: what are you trying to do? Do you want to re-tell a familiar Bible story, such as the Nativity or the Passion, and, if so, how? Is your first priority to enchant the audience with its beauty and remind them of the ancient glory of our Faith? Would you rather find a script that relates the story to our personal lives today, involving every one of us in the action through the hope of the newborn Child or our guilt for the suffering on the Cross? There are other plays which tell these stories from a new angle, making the landlady at Bethlehem into the central figure, or with slightly altered sympathies, so that Judas becomes a more attractive character. You may even prefer to revive one of the old Mystery Plays, which give the story a mediaeval flavour of raucous humour and formal verse.

Of course you are not limited to such well-known subjects as these. There are plenty of scripts about Joseph, Moses, Job, Ruth, Daniel, Hosea, St Paul. James Bridie has written a number of plays based on the Apocrypha. You do not have to have a story from the Bible. There are plenty of plays about other events in Christian history, and the lives of the Saints have been favourite subjects, especially St Thomas à Becket, St Francis of Assisi and Joan of Arc. They do not have to be Catholic. Fine plays have been written about Cranmer, Luther, Wesley and George Fox. Here again, you will find an enormous variety of approach, ranging from plays that are little more than animated stained-glass windows to difficult and disturbing texts like *Murder in the Cathedral* or such West End successes as *A Man for All Seasons*.

Many of the best Christian plays are not about church history, however, and may not always at first sight appear to be religious at all. This should not be surprising. Very few of Our Lord's parables were concerned with conventional religion; they were more often about farmers, shepherds and vinegrowers, rich men and the financial dealings of their agents, householders or their wives, engaged in the petty business of every day. Some playwrights have put these stories into a modern setting. Others have written new parables of their own. Sometimes such plays have enjoyed a successful run in the theatre without anyone recognising them for what they were.

In making your choice, you should be guided not only by what you would like to do but also by what would communicate best to your particular audience. The congregation of a country parish may have very different tastes from their counterparts in a London suburb. Students may enjoy a show which would bore workers on a factory floor. The clergy, too, may have views about what is or is not suitable for playing in church. It is not a question of playing down to popular taste - in fact you may legitimately wish to give people a shock - but you will achieve nothing if your play does not reach out to them where they are now.

Whatever play you finally choose, please remember one thing: a great many authors have to live by what they write. If you want to perform a writer's play, you *must* get permission (details of where to apply are normally given at the beginning of the script) and pay the prescribed performing fee, usually in advance. Some people, even - sad to say - some clergy, have an idea that if the performance is in church, then it doesn't really count; it is in a 'good cause', so the author ought not to expect any money. Such an attitude is not Christian. It is not even honest. To steal people's words is just as much theft as to steal their wallet. If, by any chance, an author does let you perform without fee, then that is a great act of generosity and should be publicly acknowledged to your audience.

What to do with the play now you've got it
By now your production team should exist, at least in outline, but it will do no harm to remind ourselves of its most important members

and the work they have to do. In fact a great many of the jobs overlap and are often done by a single person, but it is useful to think of them all separately, as they would be in the professional theatre.

The DIRECTOR is the person in charge of all the artistic work of the play: the one who supervises rehearsals, giving the actors guidance, encouragement and criticism, and who approves the designs, lighting and sound. The cast, the stage management and all the rest of the team are ultimately responsible to the director. In fact, this position is so important that the whole of the next two chapters will be given up to it.

Strictly speaking, the director is in turn responsible to the MANAGER, who is in charge of absolutely everything: the permissions, the presentation, the publicity, the front-of-house and the money, for even the simplest amateur production is going to cost something. In the professional theatre, the manager would normally choose the play and appoint the director, and then they would work very closely together. In your group, it is probably better that one person should do both jobs. What is needed at this stage is single-minded leadership.

(You will very commonly hear the word PRODUCER, but its disadvantage is that it is ambiguous. In films, and increasingly in the theatre, it is used to describe what we have called the manager, whereas in more traditional theatre parlance it means the director. Of course, where one person is fulfilling both functions, so that there is no question of confusion, it is an excellent job description, since it covers both meanings.)

The next most important – and certainly the busiest – person is the STAGE MANAGER, but please think carefully before trying to double this job as well. It is a big enough responsibility on its own, and in any case by this time you need someone to argue with you and tell you what can and can't be done. The stage manager (in person or through an assistant) will have a full-time job at every rehearsal, besides keeping constant control over all the backstage staff and even – during the actual performance – of the actors themselves.

If you are to have costumes, and even items of scenery, then you will need a DESIGNER and a WARDROBE MISTRESS/MASTER and perhaps a CARPENTER as well. If you have special lighting, you will need an ELECTRICIAN, and in any case someone must be responsible for switching the ordinary church lights off and on. Shows with music may need a MUSICAL DIRECTOR and a SOUND OPERATOR or MUSICIANS. If there is furniture or scenery to be shifted, some people will have to do the work of STAGEHANDS. The list is almost endless, and for the moment you had better keep it as short as you can. A great deal more will be said about the backstage community in a later chapter, but they will have to be appointed before any work on the production begins.

If necessary, a play can be performed without lights, music, costumes or scenery, but the absolutely vital members of the team are the performers, and casting should be done with great care. With a new, small group, auditions as such may not be strictly necessary. Your play should have been chosen with a view to the people available to act in it, and your experience with them in readings, workshops and theatre games should have given you some knowledge of their different capabilities. Nevertheless, it is quite a good idea to let several people read for each part. It may even give you fresh insights that you might otherwise have missed.

Do remember that auditions are a hideously nervous business for the actors, and especially for beginners. Don't ask the poor things to stand up and declaim while you and (worse still) the other aspirants stare at them woodenly from a distance. It is better to sit everybody round a table and let them all join in a reading of the whole play, changing the parts from time to time as they go. By the end you should have tried all the possible permutations of your cast and be ready to make your decisions. Moreover, all the actors will know what the whole play is about. You might be surprised to learn that otherwise some of them might never read anything but their own lines.

The one remaining resource that you have to allot is rehearsal time. The minimum that any respectable professional repertory will give to a full-length play nowadays is two weeks, which means between forty and forty-five hours, but this speed is only suitable for experienced professionals working against the clock. It is far too quick for you. By contrast, a London production will be rehearsed for anything from a hundred to two hundred hours, which you would probably find too long. Over-rehearsal can make inexperienced actors go stale.

You have one great advantage over the professional: there is plenty of time between your rehearsals. Much of an actor's preparation is a matter of allowing conscious ideas to seep gradually down into his emotional and physical centres, and this is not a quick process. You should aim to rehearse for a minimum of two and a maximum of three sessions of three hours each every week. Encourage the cast to work hard on their parts in between, but some of the work will be done for them by the mere passing of time, just as people often speak of sleeping on a problem.

How many weeks? If your play lasts up to two hours, which is a long time to ask an audience to sit on hard pews, you will need a minimum of six weeks, with a spurt over the final weekend, giving you a total rehearsal time of perhaps sixty hours. For an hour-long play, you should not drop lower than four weeks (say forty hours). Three weeks (thirty hours) will do for something of half an hour or so. People should put down their books one third of the time through rehearsal and be word-perfect for the last third.

All these questions will have to be thought out before you even order the copies of the script. You are going to put on a play in surroundings which were not intended for a theatre, and it will take every spark of your imagination to visualise all the problems. It is only too easy to reach the first night and discover some terrible snag which you had never thought of. One purpose of this book is to save you from that calamity.

The director's vision

It is the task of the director to transform the script of the play into something the audience can hear and see, something that will involve, amuse and move them, so that they become drawn for the moment into another time and place. The play may, of course, do a great deal more to them than that: it may inform them of things they never knew, it may cause them to look at familiar scenes and situations in an entirely new light, and it may even effect some fundamental change in their lives. If it does these things, however, that will be largely due to the content of the script, whereas the director's job is merely to bring that script to life.

If you are directing a play, therefore, your first duty is to read the script and study it carefully. This may seem obvious, but it is a job that is very seldom done as thoroughly as it should be. Some directors even make the grave mistake of trying to visualise the production before they have really studied the script at all, so that they spend most of their rehearsals in an effort to bend the text to fit their interpretation. When this happens, the play that is finally shown to the audience is a strangely mutilated and unbalanced affair, probably full of the director's favourite tricks but totally lacking the inner meaning of the original.

Reading and studying the script should begin well before the first rehearsal – indeed, well before the casting – but it should not stop before the first performance. There is far more to be dug out of a script of quality than can be found at first sight, and you may very well go on making new discoveries every day. Even an indifferent play can go on yielding surprises. The theatre is an organic thing, and its characters are genuine creations rather than merely manufactured objects. Even the author may not fully understand the people whose lines he has written, and you will learn more and more about them not only in rehearsals but also by studying the text.

Yes, but what are you to look for? How do you set about disentangling the author's intention from this bewildering maze of words? Should you try to understand its intellectual content, do you concentrate on the practical problems, or are you simply concerned with feelings? Do you begin by working out the moves, or is it better to start with the meaning of the spoken word and let the actions emerge instinctively during rehearsal? Is it the underlying truth of the play you should be after, or the theatrical effect? Should you aim at a mechanically perfect show, where everybody moves and speaks with parade-ground efficiency or is the real purpose to create a new atmosphere in which the play unfolds like a flower? The answer is, of course, that you want to achieve all of these, and the only remaining question is, where do you begin?

In the first instance, it is probably best to read the play as you would read a story, letting the author set light to your imagination. When we read a novel, we hear voices and see pictures in our heads, and a good play should have the same effect. At this stage, don't make any attempt to pin it down to the practicalities of performance; just let it happen in your mind, as if you were watching a film. On the first reading, some passages may do this for you, others may not. Don't assume that this means that some parts of the play are better than others; the fault may very well lie in your own understanding. Simply make a note of the bits that didn't automatically work for you. These are going to need special attention later on.

Going through the script again, look for the main climaxes of the action. In every play there are moments of increased tension – it may be of excitement, emotion or comedy – and these are the parts which the audience will particularly remember. Mark these passages as you find them (pencil, please, if it's a hired script!) and try to decide which are the most important. Your whole production should be shaped to lead up to such moments and to make them as striking as possible when they come. The tension builds up, the explosion comes, and then we all relax until the tension starts to build again. No audience can react to a play that is all tension, any more than to a piece of music all in double forte; they will simply grow numb to the effect. The way to reach them is through variety – in pace, in volume, in emotion, in activity – and this should spring from the natural rise and fall of the script. As you continue studying the text, you will gradually find that the play is a series of tiny, articulated sections, each with its gathering momentum, climax and release.

Imagine a short play based on the Prodigal Son. In the first scene we see the family at a meal in the farmhouse. The Prodigal asks if he can have his share of the inheritance. Instantly tension has begun. The Father is worried about whether he will squander it. The Elder Brother says the boy is of no use on the farm anyway. The Mother is distressed at the thought of his leaving home and feels he is too young to manage on his own; but with the typical charm of a younger child the Prodigal talks her round. He cuts little ice, however, with the surly old Farmhand, who has come in for orders and instantly sides with the Elder Brother. Finally the Father gives way: all right, the boy can have the money. The Prodigal is thrilled, embraces his Mother and Father and runs off excitedly. His Father goes to make the necessary arrangements, the Elder Brother and the Farmhand comment resentfully on the fact that it is always the young one who gets the attention, and finally the Mother is left, a little tearful now, to clear up the meal on her own.

In that scene the overall pattern is very simple. The tension begins when the Prodigal makes his request and builds up steadily as the others join in, like the winding up of a clockwork spring. The climax comes when the Father agrees; everybody reacts with their own characteristic emotion, and the scene settles down again to an uneasy calm. In planning the moves, therefore, the director should keep that moment constantly in mind, arranging the actors so that everyone's attention will be solidly on the Father as he makes his decision. The excitement and movement should also grow busier and noisier as the climax approaches and die away again afterwards.

This brings us to another point which the Director must look out for: the distinction between scenes that should be BUSY and those that should be CALM. This is not to be confused with the alternation of tension and relaxation which we have just been considering. In the first scene of our imaginary play, the noise and the tension built up together, and so did the release and the quiet, but this is not always the case. Let us imagine the second scene in our play, *The Prodigal Son*.

Scene Two is set in a distant and corrupt city to which our hero has travelled with his money, which he is spending like water on every vice he can find. The lights, the noise, the glamour fascinate him. Mysterious women beckon from the shadows, convivial acquaintances ply him with drink and cheat him at gambling, street hawkers dazzle him with tawdry trinkets, burly strangers pester him for a loan. All the bustle of Vanity Fair whirls round him. Slowly he is drawn under the spell of a young beauty who lures him into a quiet corner out of sight of the crowd, where two thieves briskly strip him of all his remaining money, and the three of them melt away, leaving him stunned and silent. In desperation, he runs back into the crowd, crying, 'Stop Thief!' but nobody takes any notice of him, except occasionally to laugh. Now that he cannot pay his bill, the innkeeper refuses to let him back into his room to collect his possessions, and he is thrown, utterly destitute, out on the street.

This scene is in total contrast to the last one. The general tempo is fast, the noise level high, and the stage should buzz with continual activity. As the climax approaches, the noise and action die away. Like the young man, we must enter that alley in silent and breathless suspense, and the robbery should be committed in stealthy dumbshow. It is followed by a terrible moment of stillness, while the boy takes in the full extent of his catastrophe. Then, as he bursts out into the crowd, all the clamour begins again, the laughter, shouts and movement, up till the moment when he is kicked out of the inn to the roars of the bystanders and limps unhappily away. This scene is like a reversed image of the first; against a background of uproar, the climax is the quietest moment.

Both these first two scenes have been EXTERNAL in nature, primarily concerned with outside events and the interaction of people upon one another. There are, of course, internal struggles going on, but they are not what interest us most. We do not ask what the Father is thinking of his younger son's request; we simply want to know whether he will agree. We notice the resentment of the Elder Brother and the old Farmhand, but mainly because they may affect the decision. When the Mother is left sadly clearing up the meal, we cannot stop to spare her much sympathy. We may even feel inclined to laugh, partly because we are relieved to have reached a decision, and partly because the silly woman seems to be crying at having her own way. That is a very superficial view, and we may look back on it differently later, but just now we are too excited to look deeply. The second scene is even more external. The strangers in the street are interesting only so far as they attract or threaten the young man. The climax in the alley is very much a matter of events: what will he do with this young woman? who are these two lurking shadows? We do not need to ask psychological questions, because our instinctive reflexes are engaged.

The third scene of our play is entirely different. There is, of course, some outward speech and action – no dramatic scene can exist without them – but this time our interest is centred in the boy's mind. He is begging at a street corner, and everybody refuses him. The weather has turned cold, and his clothes are inadequate. There is a famine, the passers-by clutch their burdens protectively. They ignore the young beggar or give him an ugly answer. Somebody spits on him. He cringes up to a young woman, who gives one look at him, gasps and shrinks away. Bent and dejected, he approaches a tough landowner, who offers him a job feeding swine. He draws himself up with wounded dignity – 'I am an orthodox Jew' – but, as the man shrugs and walks away, his pride fails him, and he runs and takes the heavy sack of husks. Desperate with hunger, he glances round to make sure no one is watching him, then dips his hand into the sack and lifts some of the pigfood to his mouth. At that moment, he has a poignant vision of his innocent and happy life on the home farm. He will go back, but how can he? He is ruined, disgraced, an object of horror. Perhaps his Father will take him on as a farm labourer. Anything would be better than his present plight.

This scene will need quite different handling from the first two. In them, we saw the Prodigal Son in relation to and sometimes in conflict with other people, but now his occasional encounters only emphasise that he is utterly alone. The real action is going on INSIDE the boy himself, and the audience must be drawn into it, while the other characters remain on the periphery. There is no noise or pace about this scene; the crisis is reached slowly and agonisingly in the mind. At the same time, the interest of the audience must never droop. You have no special effects or sudden events to help you here. Everything depends on the simplicity and inward sincerity of the central character. The actor must not indulge himself with a shred of self-pity, but our emotions must be torn for him as we watch, and that moment of quiet decision is the real turning-point of the play.

Realising that no audience can keep up an emotion for too long, our imaginary author has decided that Scene Four is the moment to introduce a note of COMEDY. We are back at the farmhouse, where a Friend has arrived with news from the great city. He has seen the Prodigal at the height of his extravagance, pouring out money like water and indulging in every vice. Everything he relates increases the horror of the Mother and Father. He believes himself to be wholly sympathetic, but he is evidently enjoying the effect he is making, and, while describing some of the boy's worst outrages, has difficulty in keeping the smile off his face. Recent news he has none: the boy has disappeared, very possibly dead. The Mother sits almost hypnotised, hearing her worst fears described in hideous detail. The Father goes to the doorway and stares out. In the distance he sees a bedraggled figure making its way to the farm. The boy is coming home.

This is the moment to say a word about the dangers and temptations of COMEDY and TRAGEDY. Too many productions treat them as if they were entirely separate and incompatible ideas, but, if tragedy and comedy cannot live together in the same scene, then there is something wrong with your concept of one or both. During the rehearsal of a scene from *Anne Frank* a very great director once said to us: 'Darlings, this is a tragedy: make me laugh.' The remark was not as perverse as it sounds, though it may take a long time to get used to what it is saying. Both ideas are, or should be, reflections of the same truth, and some of the finest drama partakes of both at once. The films of Charley Chaplin constantly teeter on the edge of tragedy, whereas the mad scene in *Lear* is played against a weird comic counterpoint.

The twin dangers are, of course, to miss your laughs or to get them in the wrong places, but, like many other forms of danger, they are easier to avoid if you do not think too much about them. Keep your eye fixed on the truth of the scene; then the laughs will play themselves, and the serious moments will command the respect of the audience. Moreover, the humour will save the tragedy from growing pompous, while the feeling will strengthen the force of the audience's escape into laughter. You will not make us feel sorry for the Prodigal in his misery unless your comic sense is used to pare the scene of all pretentiousness, and the Friend will fail to make us laugh unless we share the distress of the Father and Mother.

Now, at the end of Scene Four, feeling and laughter meet head on. The Father has seen his son in the distance and comes to tell the good news to his wife, but the neighbour never lets him get it out. Gradually the audience realises what he is trying to say, which makes the Mother's misery more touching and the neighbour's pessimism more absurd. This is the comic crisis of the scene, and it bursts when the starved and ragged Prodigal almost falls in at the door. For a long moment the others gape at him in silence, while the audience's laughter fades away and they take in his wretched appearance. Then, quietly and humbly, he starts his appeal.

He only gets through the first sentence before his Father springs back to life. Calling for fresh clothes, he lifts the boy to his feet and hugs him. Farmhands and dairymaids run in excitedly. The Mother is wondering what on earth they can give the boy to eat – the lamb is practically finished, and she was going to make a stew – when the Father dumbfounds her by giving orders to slaughter the prize calf. The Friend, gulping down his disappointment, would like to offer some serious advice, but nobody listens to him, somebody starts playing an instrument, and dancing breaks out. The play seems set for a happy ending, but we are not through yet.

The last scene reminds us that things are not completely solved. Out in the fields the Elder Brother is coming home after another day's work, when he hears the music and dancing. Along comes the old Farmhand from the first scene. (Why? The author gives no explanation of his entrance. How can we make it seem natural? Perhaps he could carry a bucket, as if busy on some task. The director will often have to ask questions like that, but don't be too quick about it; the reason may emerge later, or we may find a better one.) The Elder Brother asks him what the noise means, and the old man explains in bitter phrases, rousing all his hearer's latent jealousy, and finally holds up a gorgeous coat: he had been sent to get this for the young Prodigal. (Ah! Now we know what he was doing there and can get rid of that bucket.) That coat is the final insult. After a few growled exchanges, the Farmhand stumps off into the house, while the Brother is turning back towards the fields again, when his Father comes running out, begging him to join in the fun. At this, the young man lets loose the resentment of years: he has never been given a party for his friends after all his faithful labour, while this young scoundrel (he will not even refer to him as his brother) has only to come back from his dissipations to be treated like a hero.

The climax of this scene is in two stages. It builds up to the moment when the Elder Brother refuses to go into the house, and at that tension it remains until his outburst to his Father. The time in between is like the pause before the axe falls, and every word, every action, is under its shadow. The angry speech takes the Father unawares, but he is too happy to feel anything but sympathy. Patiently he reassures the sulky young man, explains how relieved his Mother feels, and finally, by describing the tiresome Friend, coaxes him into a reluctant smile. They go into the feast together, the Father's arm round the shoulders of his Elder Son, and we have reached the end of the play.

Of course it has not been presented to us like that. The script consists of dialogue, with or without stage directions. You will need to read it over and over again before the shape emerges so clearly, and some speeches can be interpreted in more than one way. Take this passage from Scene One:

FATHER: Have you thought about your poor mother? How is she going to feel when you've gone?

PRODIGAL: You'll understand, won't you, Mother? After all, I'm not a child any longer. I'm a grown man.

MOTHER: I don't know, dear. It's not just a question of age. You are still very young in your ways.

PRODIGAL: That's it, Mother dear. I need to get away, stand on my own feet. Then I shall be able to find myself. You understand.

BROTHER: It's about time he grew up.

FATHER: And your elder brother – what about him? One pair of hands less, and he's worked off his feet as it is.

BROTHER: Oh, don't worry about me. I can manage.

PRODIGAL: There you are!

FATHER: I'm not so sure. A farm like this needs a lot of work to keep it going.

MOTHER: The farm's not the most important thing though, is it? Do let's think first about our boy.

PRODIGAL: Oh, please don't call me that, Mother!

FATHER: I'm trying to think of everyone, dear.

PRODIGAL: Look, it's my one chance. I'll never make my way in the world if I don't start young.

MOTHER (*to* FATHER): There's something in what he says, dear. You were very young when you started, and look how well you've done.

FATHER: Yes, but I didn't have any choice. I was thrown out on the world with nothing but my two hands.

PRODIGAL: Well then, I ought to do even better. I'll have the money, to give me a flying start.

MOTHER: You won't do anything silly with it, will you? Please promise me that.

FATHER: And I'm still worried about your brother.

BROTHER: I don't want to stop him, if he wants to go. As you say, there'll be a bit more work for me, but he won't make all that difference.

FARMHAND: There's one young man here who isn't afraid of work.

FATHER: We're none of us afraid of work, Reuben. We're just trying to agree what's the best way to set about things.

Here is one of those tiny sections, more or less complete in itself, which, together with a series of others before and after, make up the whole scene. It is of course a very simple passage, but do not feel that it is an insult to be asked to read it through several times. Study the movement within each character. The Mother in particular seems to change her viewpoint during the scene. Why? Does the Father shift his ground at all? What do you think of the Elder Brother's attitude? Do we learn anything from the Farmhand's comment, and why do you think he makes it? You may also detect a change in the Father's confidence; is he gaining or losing command of the situation? There is no obvious sudden crisis in this passage, but nevertheless something has happened, there has been development in these few lines. Try to detect where and how it happened, look for the lines that changed the situation and plot the emotional rise and fall. Listen to the lines in your head and try to hear whether each should be quiet or noisy, quick or slow. On a larger scale, this is what you will have to do with the whole play.

When you have grown really conversant with the play, it should run like a film on the imaginary television set in your mind. At each reading the focus will grow a little clearer. You will know when it is loud or soft, fast or slow, you will recognise the moments of rising tension, the climaxes, the relaxations, and you will have detected the secret hinges of the story. When you have done all this, you have only begun. You have your vision, but now you must translate it into what you can do with your limited resources, your actors, your stage management and your stage.

Fitting it into the church

Up till now, your vision of the play has been limited by nothing but the scope of your own imagination. You may have seen the farmhouse in Scene One as a whitewashed cube, shimmering in the heat of first-century Judaea, or as an oak-beamed manor in modern Sussex. In Scene Two, the city streets could stretch as far as you pleased, crowded with endless passers-by and noisy with the din of traffic and the tinkle of music. You may have envisaged the characters in glittering robes or simple homespun. Perhaps you have translated the whole thing into the present day and seen your hero in jeans.

Whatever the picture you have created, it is likely to suffer something of a jar when you try to squeeze it into the resources at your disposal – the space, the budget and (above all) the human beings. Somehow you have got to turn your vision into an actual production, so that the audience can glimpse something of it too; so we had better begin by looking at some of the brute facts we may suppose you have to cope with.

For a start, you had better take a long, serious look at the acting area. Let us say you are to perform in a suburban parish church, which was built in 1883. It has a wooden roof (good!) and is designed in the architect's interpretation of the Decorated Period, with north and south aisles, separated from the nave by wide gothic arcades. Four steps lead up into the chancel, which is largely filled with choir stalls, opening out again to the sanctuary and Communion Table beyond. The last vicar removed a wrought iron screen at the top of the steps, but the stone base proved too much for him and still projects about a foot above the chancel floor. The pulpit more or less conceals the chancel from anyone sitting in the north aisle, and the brass eagle lectern takes four strong men to move. The vestries are on the south side of the choir and give access to both the sanctuary and to the crossing, just to the west of the chancel arch. There is an aisle down the centre of the nave, so that nobody can sit in what might be the best seats of all. The only two outside doors that actually work are in the south-west corner and from the choir vestry. By a stroke of luck, there was a big ecumenical occasion about five years ago, for which one of the congregation, who is good at that sort of thing, made a platform which fits over the chancel steps and spreads out in a sort of narrow mantelpiece, two feet high, four feet deep and twelve feet wide, in front of the stone base of the vanished screen. When you finally track it down in the boiler-room, it is slightly damaged and filthy. Nevertheless, with hard work it can be restored to service.

At this point, it is worth reminding you that you will get nowhere at all unless you succeed in wooing the verger, caretaker or whoever is responsible for the fabric of the church. That platform will have to be scrupulously cleaned before it can be brought in, and all sorts of promises will have to be given (and believed!) about your respect for the carpets, stone and woodwork. Moreover, the church must be totally unimpeded for the Sunday services immediately before your perform-ance, and the platform is too heavy and awkward to put up more than once, which means that up till very nearly the last moment rehearsals will have to take place on the flat, imagining what it will be like on the night. In the same way, you cannot move the eagle till the last moment, so you will have to rehearse round it, pretending that it isn't there. It would be nice to move the pulpit as well, but that proves to be fixed to the stonework, so you will have to make the best of it.

Now have a look at the money. Each member of your drama group has been invited to contribute a pound towards the production, and most of them have done so, even including Sharon, who is only just sixteen and whom you hardly liked to ask. This means you have nineteen pounds, and the church council have nobly stumped up pound for pound, so the total has doubled to thirty-eight. For a brief moment you feel quite rich. Then you remember that the royalties are four pounds per performance, and you are planning to do it twice. Eight pounds gone, thirty to go. Then you had hoped to put posters in all the local churches. The organist's daughter is marvellous at lettering, and the photocopy shop will do A3 at 25 pence a go. There are twelve churches within easy reach; some of them may want to have two. Then there are the library, the schools, some of the shops . . . say forty altogether, and there's another ten pounds gone. We're down to twenty. A5 handbills would be nice too, and this time we are luckier; the man who duplicates the church notices has offered to do them at cost. Five hundred handbills for four pounds, and we still have sixteen pounds for all the expenses of the production. Do we really want to do it in costume? After reading the script again and again, you cannot find a single line that could not have been said today, so let's do the play in modern dress. Better save where we can. A pound a head wasn't so much after all.

Now take a look at the most important asset of all: the people. For the moment let us forget the stage staff, though they must be considered right from the beginning. What matters first is the cast.

The play lists nine named characters: The Father, the Mother, the Prodigal, his Elder Brother, the Farmhand, the Mysterious Woman, the Inn-Keeper, the Pig-breeder and the Friend. Then it goes on, rather tiresomely, to talk about Bystanders, Hawkers, Thieves, Dairy-Maids, Labourers ... there seems to be no end to them. If we press all the Stage Staff to come onstage at one moment or another we can just raise nine men and eight women, ranging from young Sharon, who doesn't want to say any lines, to Herbert, aged at least seventy, who is only too willing.

With these, we shall be hard-pressed to manage. There are no fewer than seven named men. What was our author thinking about to write so few parts for women? The Father, the Prodigal, the Brother and the Friend will use up the only ones we could really describe as actors, but old Herbert will enjoy the Farmhand, and he certainly is a great character. The two thieves can be masked, so they can double with the Elder Brother and the Father. The Inn-Keeper is such a small part that perhaps we can give it to Gordon, the electrician, and perhaps Jeff, the assistant stage manager, could have a go at the Pig-breeder, but we shall have to clear both of those with Norah; as stage manager, she has first call on the backstage staff. One thing is certain: she won't be able to spare either of them at the end, so all the extras in the last scene will have to be women.

The Mother is no problem, because one thing our group is really strong on is middle-aged women. (In fact, if Norah won't let us have Jeff, we might change the sex of the Pig-breeder and give the part to Sibyl, who is also chairperson of the church Finance Committee and can be quite formidable when she wants to be.) The real difficulty is the Mysterious Woman in Scene Two, largely because all our actresses are known to the whole congregation and do not seem mysterious in the least. It's no good considering Sharon, because – quite apart from the lines – her mother would undoubtedly put her foot down. On balance, we shall have to settle for Dilys, who is twenty-three. She is not as glamorous as we might have wished, being what the Vicar would call a 'nice, wholesome girl', but she came up surprisingly well at the reading. She and Sharon will have to come back as dairymaids for the party. Indeed, we shall need to use everybody for the crowd scenes.

Now we shall have to start on the plotting, that is to say the position and movements of every single performer, property and piece of furniture. Directors vary enormously in how they set about this. Some work out every detail before the first rehearsal, others think entirely on their feet, but neither of these courses is very suitable for any but the most experienced. The trouble with doing it all in advance is that it is very difficult to visualise, though you can help yourself by making a cardboard model of the acting area and moving chessmen or toy soldiers about on it. Once you get real, live people to do your moves, however, they will look curiously different from your model, so that all your carefully laid plans may come to dust.

On the other hand, making it all up as you go along is an even greater risk. You may find you have wound your actors into a knot from which it is impossible to extricate them without going back to the beginning and starting all over again. Needless to say, this will not be popular with your cast or stage management, but that is the least of your troubles. The first plotting makes an important impression on an actor's mind and gives him a comforting discipline within which to work. If it is all suddenly reversed, he will be badly unsettled. He may easily get muddled, and his faith in the director will be shaken.

The best course is to work out your general picture in fairly broad outline, while keeping the finer details to be worked out in the early rehearsals. Naturally, you will find you have made mistakes, which you have to go back and correct, but on this system they ought not to be very grave ones. For this reason it is often wiser to introduce your instructions with some such phrase as 'Let's try it this way,' than to say baldly, 'This is what I want you to do.' It is also vital that the stage manager or assistant stage manager should sit at the book for every rehearsal, clearly recording every move. You will be very lucky if at some time the actors don't get into a disagreement about where they ought to be, and that is when the prompt copy needs to be an infallible authority. In fact, if the stage manager sees somebody making a wrong move at a rehearsal, he or she should let the director know at the first convenient moment.

Let us have a go at plotting the first scene of *The Prodigal*. The author calmly announces: 'The family are seated at a meal.' Instantly you are in trouble. Being in church, you have no front curtain to hide the actors coming on. And what about the table? How is it going to get there, and – worse – how is it going to get off again? Nevertheless we do want a table; a meal would look silly without one. It will just have to be in place when the audience come in, and we will worry about moving it later. The chairs can be onstage as well, and we shall need four of them. The bigger problem is, how do we begin the scene?

Wait a minute! Suppose the Mother laid the cloth! We don't need much; a soup tureen, ladle and four deep soup bowls and spoons will give the idea of a meal clearly enough. It's evident from the text that the men expect her to wait on them, so we can establish something about the family and their relationship before a word has been spoken. Then the Father can come in, sit down, look at his watch – where are the boys? – and tap his fingers on the table. The Elder Brother comes in wearing gumboots, still wiping his newly-washed hands on his corduroys. Catching a look from his Mother, he sighs, slips off the gumboots and puts on a pair of slippers: (stage manager, please note: slippers to be set by chair). They are all waiting in their chairs when the Prodigal bounces in, late as usual, makes peace with a winning smile and sits down. Father mumbles a grace, and Mother serves the meal. (Do we want real food? Probably not, but let's make a few experiments at later rehearsals.) Now the scene can begin.

When four people sit at a table, they normally sit on all four sides. Any other arrangement, even in Leonardo's Last Supper, looks a little odd. Besides, our table will have to be too small for everyone to crowd round the upstage side, so at least one person is going to have to sit with his back more or less to the audience. We can mitigate the situation by setting the table at an angle, so that no one faces straight upstage. The most important people in this scene are the Father, who has to make the decision, and the Prodigal, who is asking him to do it, so they had better sit on the two upstage sides, facing more or less out front, while the Mother and Elder Brother sit opposite to them. The Mother can bob conveniently up and down to clear the sightlines now and then, and the Farmhand, when he comes in, can stand upstage of the table, which, incidentally won't go onto our narrow little apron stage, so it will have to be set at the mouth of the chancel, in front of the choir stalls. Fortunately the clergy seats are held down by nothing more impregnable than four No 12 screws, so we shall be able to take them out for the performance.

There is very little physical action, particularly from the Father and Elder Brother, but it may be a good thing if the Prodigal bounces about in his excitement, and the busy Mother can provide us with some movement. Pace, noise and action build up the tension to the moment when the Father finally says Yes. That might be a good moment for him to stand, so as to top his active wife and importunate son. There is a moment of suspense – he agrees – and instantly the Prodigal is off again, kissing his Mother, shaking hands with his Father and slapping his Elder Brother on the back. He can even have a go at the Farmhand, though he will surely get very little change out of him. So off he goes, while his Father and Brother go their different ways, leaving his Mother wistfully clearing the table. The author just wrote 'Curtain', but we can still get something out of the scene. Let the Elder Brother offer to carry the tray, so that, when she refuses, we can glimpse that she is trying to hide her tears.

For Scene Two we shall want an instant and total change. If we can run to lighting effects, this is an obvious moment for them. The designer has come up with an interesting idea; what about suspending a Chinese lantern above the stage, which can be switched on now, while all the other lights are lowered? Music would be effective too. Shall we play a cassette, or even have somebody whistling? It is tempting to ask the organist if he could play some ragtime, but this might be a risky experiment. The organ is a very big instrument, which could easily drown the whole show, and the organist may not wish you to be the one who calls the tune. Noting down all these possibilities, we begin to plot the action.

Clearly the most important place is the dark alley where the Prodigal is going to be robbed, so we must fix that first. The most obvious site is the far end of the choir, but that is not very visible from a lot of pews because of the position of the pulpit. If possible, we want to avoid the bit of stage we used for the meal in Scene One (for one thing, we never took away the table) but on the otherside of the chancel we're in trouble with the pulpit again. To play that sequence on the apron would destroy the sense of secrecy, so where ... Perhaps we could put the robbery right in the middle of the audience itself, in that wasted centre aisle. Let's try it anyway, and then the apron can be the street.

Once again, we have to set the scene gradually, and it is often best to bring the actors on one at a time, so that the audience can take each of them in. Of course, you don't usually see a table beside a street, unless ... unless ... what about a three-card-trick man? Perhaps Norah will spare us Jeff after all, but we'll still have Sibyl for the Pig-breeder. There's Jeff, playing his cards, 'Now you see her, now you don't, come along, my lucky friends – ' and at once the audience will know exactly where they are. Now Sandra (thirty-one) high-heels across the apron, pausing to turn over one of Jeff's cards – he winks at her – and finally leaning against the pulpit and beginning to do something to her nails. We have succeeded in talking Sid, the carpenter, into playing the Burly Cadger, on the promise that he never has to say a word. Now he comes on from the right, passes Sandra, turns back and whispers to her. She sniggers, and he moves slowly left, as Margaret (fifty-four) comes down between the choir stalls, shaking her fist at him. For a moment he seems inclined to make an issue of it, but at this moment Helen (nineteen) runs on and whispers to him, pointing back the way she has come. The Prodigal is about to enter. Instantly they stiffen, like cats sighting a bird. At last we are ready to begin the scene. All that we have done so far was covered by the opening stage direction: 'A disreputable street, with thieves, hawkers, etc. Enter the Prodigal.'

For a time, the text more or less plays itself, as Sid whines and then threatens the Prodigal, who goes on to lose handfuls of banknotes over Jeff's three-card-trick. (The thing about stage banknotes is to get the paper quality right. Then a splash of the right colour will do all you need.) Meanwhile, Dilys, with her hair down and dressed in something glittering, moves silently up the darkened aisle from the back of the church. The audience are only just aware of her, as she stands with her back to them, staring at her prey. When she speaks to him, we hear her voice, but it is the boy whom we watch. Leading him on, she backs slowly down the aisle, while he follows, as if in a trance. The others slowly come to rest, watching the drama unfold. In the half dark, the two thieves come running up from the back. We hear a scuffle – a blow – a cry – and then the Prodigal staggers back into the light, with his shirt open and his coat pulled off one shoulder. The audience have seen the robbery in their imagination, where it will have been much more vivid than anything we could have put on the stage. And now the Innkeeper is coming down to the mouth of the chancel to present the poor victim with his bill.

Perhaps we don't need to make any very clear division between Scenes Two and Three. After the Innkeeper has thrown him out, the rest of the cast laugh and leave him to his fate. Admittedly the script says, 'Exit the Prodigal', but what is the point, when the next scene begins: 'A Street: Enter the Prodigal'? Why not just leave him there, painfully climbing to his feet, and start again without a pause? Yes, but not so fast! His clothes ought to be more ragged now, and there are lines in the script about feeling the cold. In any case, time must have passed in order for him to feel hungry. We need a gap of sorts.

The costume change shouldn't be too difficult. Sid, as the Burly Cadger, could pull the coat off him when the Innkeeper flings him into the street, leaving him a shirt with torn and ragged sleeves. (Surely, somebody must have an old shirt they don't mind ruining.) But wouldn't that look a bit funny? Why should his shirt be ragged already? All right, then suppose at that moment we turn out all the lights except something at the far end of the sanctuary, so that the cast can leave in silhouette, and, when the lights come up again, our bright young spark will have turned into a beggar. We might even enhance the sense of time passing by a slow drum beat. (The fleshy part of your fist pounding on a piece of the oak panelling makes a wonderfully impressive noise.) To emphasise that winter is come, all the others can come on huddled in greatcoats, which will also help to disguise the fact that we are using the same people over again.

In Scene Three the author has rather tiresomely given his hero a number of monologues, interspersed with unsuccessful attempts at begging. It felt all right when we read it; the lines are natural enough, but how is the actor to deliver them? In real life, he would probably have muttered them under his breath, but, if he does that in church, nobody will hear a word. On the other hand, if he delivers them like Shakespearian soliloquies, won't that destroy the naturalistic style we have been trying so hard to build up? Should he talk to the audience, or to himself, or even, conceivably, to God? Would it make sense for him to try and beg from the front rows and then confide in them? Or shall we keep the lectern after all and try for a weird effect by letting him talk to the Eagle?

The truth is that these questions are impossible to answer in advance, because they depend entirely on your actor. Whenever you plan a move or hear a line in your head, you must always remember that you may have to modify your ideas if you are to get the best out of your cast. The director who behaves like a puppeteer must not be surprised if the actors respond by behaving as if they were made out of wood. You are there not to bully your cast but to find what they can do best and woo them into doing it better. Most of all this is true of INTERNAL acting, and in this long and almost solitary scene you may have to try a number of experiments before you find the right way for your particular actor to do it.

On the other hand, you must give the actors a firm lead. Standing on the stage, thinking of the audience who will soon be staring at them, they feel desperately vulnerable and need every kind of support, pathetically anxious to please you in the hope that you can protect them from the displeasure of the audience. So don't ask them how they want to play the scene. Say: 'Look, I think it will work best this way.' Then, if it doesn't, you must be ready with another wonderful idea. And all the time you must watch them at work, so that you can play up their strengths and conceal their weaknesses.

By comparison, Scene Four is a walkover. For the part of the Family Friend you have saved Desmond (forty-seven and the Dame in the local pantomime) because you knew that with his experience he could be sure of making them laugh. Give him the centre of the stage and let him loose, but always bear in mind that this scene is leading up to the return of the Prodigal. We are back in the farmhouse of course, just behind that low wall and round the table. We need above all to see the Father's face, when he sees his son in the distance, so the easiest way will be to let the boy come up the centre aisle, so that the Father can come to the front of the stage to see him. That aisle is proving rather a blessing after all.

We shall have to let the party sweep right up to the far end of the chancel in order to leave room for that bitter last scene. Everybody can be drawn into it, except for Sid, the electrician, and Jeff, the ASM, who are going to be busy. The other characters from Scenes Two and Three have had plenty of time to change, and we need a real explosion of festivity. We ought to have some music too, but, if all else fails, they can sing. Very soon, however, that will all have to die away to silence and continue in distant dumbshow after the entrance of the Elder Brother. Better not bring him on from the same direction as the Prodigal. Better if he comes past the pulpit, so that the Farmhand can meet him, coming from the other side.

Here's a problem! What about that coat which the Father has told the Farmhand to bring? Somehow we failed to think about that when we decided to go modern, but what sort of clothes could they be today? Well, the answer's not so difficult as it might have been fifty years ago. Somebody's bound to have a bright velvet jacket and perhaps a frilly shirt, and maybe the Prodigal could even disappear and slip into them and come back again into the party without the audience ever noticing he'd been away. So the Farmhand can take them upstage to the party, and the Father can come down to the Elder Brother for their final confrontation.

It seems a pity right at the end to have everyone crowded away in the distance, so perhaps, when the Father and Son turn to go indoors, the party could come out to meet them, the music rising up again to full volume, and they could spin away down the aisles, laughing and dancing as they go.

These directions will not be of any immediate use to you, as they are intended for a play that does not exist, unless you choose to write it, but they may illustrate the general principle that you must fit your production to your surroundings. The practical difficulties of playing in church are often immense, but they can most easily be overcome if you do not try to work against the grain of the building. There are also great compensations. The beauty, the atmosphere will do wonders for your production, if only you will allow them to work for you. The great thing is to study your surroundings and appreciate the difficulties and advantages they have to offer.

Do we have to have all these rehearsals?

'I've learnt my lines and I know my moves; do I have to come to rehearsals after this?' It's rather like saying, 'I've got my box of paints and I've set up my canvas; do I really have to paint the picture?' Learning lines and moves are technical skills without which we cannot have a performance at all, but they are only the groundwork on which a performance is to be built. When you come to think about it, there are different degrees of learning. It is possible to know your lines well enough to be able to write them down, or even to visualise them on the page of your script. But that isn't at all the same thing as knowing them so well that you can say them without thinking about them – saying them just as if they were lines inside your own head. And that is what acting is about – saying your lines as if they were not 'lines' at all, but real thoughts which had sprung into your mind for the first time at the moment when you speak them. This applies to 'moves', too. A move can look purely mechanical, as if the actor is crossing from upstage right to downstage left just because the director has told him or her to move that way. All moves should spring from an inner impulsion. Make sure you know just *why* your character is making that 'move'. If you can't work if out, then discuss it with your director and discover the motive.

Until 'lines' and 'moves' spring from inside your character, no amount of accurate memorising will convince the audience that a real event is taking place on the stage. This is why rehearsals should go on long after the memorising has taken place. The actor needs time to allow for the sub-consciousness to take over the part he or she is playing so that it can be expressed with a minimum of conscious thought. This can only happen when the 'lines' have been learnt so thoroughly that the actor is not exercised by the thought, 'What do I say next?'

All acting is about spontaneity, about thinking and feeling for the first time. And it is perhaps the most difficult thing to achieve. It is possible, of course, to waste your rehearsal time because you haven't 'worked' on the notes given to you by your director. Your part won't become spontaneous merely by repetition. It will need much imaginative thought at every stage of rehearsal, and you won't find your character growing unless you are prepared to spend time studying it at home as well as during rehearsals.

If you are the director, and especially if you are working with a company who can only meet once or twice a week, and probably after their working hours, you won't want to waste a moment of precious rehearsal time. Make sure that your company are punctual. If one member should arrive five minutes late, he or she may have cost the rest of the company five minutes for each of them. Say there are eight of them waiting that five minutes – then they will have wasted forty minutes between them. Late-comers who are adept at finding excuses may become a little more chary of being unpunctual once this piece of arithmetic has been pointed out.

Don't waste the first twenty minutes of your rehearsal time with coffee and gossip. It's much more helpful to take a break after you have been going an hour and a half. Your cast may be flagging and the coffee necessary. By then they will probably want to talk about the play instead of what happened to them in the office, factory, farm or school, or wherever they may have come from.

As director you will have to judge just when to move from one stage of rehearsal to the next. It's always advisable to have at least two readings of the play before your rehearsals begin at all. Let the first reading be followed by a general discussion of the play. It's important for everyone to share the same views as to what the play is about and the relationships of the characters to each other. Having reached agreement about this (and the director's views must be paramount), the second reading will be affected by this agreement and the director will be able to give notes when it is over; the actors will go home with a lot to think about.

You will probably want to use your next three or four rehearsals for the purpose of 'blocking'. This means the arranging of moves in connection with the furniture and the set. Always use makeshift furniture if you haven't got the real thing for the rehearsal period. As director, you may have arranged the 'moves' on paper, but you will probably find they don't all work out as happily as you had charted them and you will need to make alterations on the floor. Always allow time for your cast to write every move down in their scripts as soon as they are given. The stage manager should be writing every move down as well. Because moves can be changed, even quite late on during the production, it's advisable always to use pencil. Every actor, and the stage manager, should bring a pencil and a rubber with them to every rehearsal.

Once the 'blocking' has taken place you would be wise to allow your actors to come to the next two or three rehearsals with books in their hands, but the sooner they can dispense with books the better. It's almost impossible to gain much from rehearsals when hands are inhibited by holding scripts. Some actors are naturally good about learning their lines, but you will have to use tact and judgment with some of the others. Basically there are two types who cling to their books. The first are so sure of themselves that they don't bother to learn their lines till the last moment. You will need to be quite brutal with these over-confident ones and ban the use of books at a given time. Once they have stumbled over lines in front of their fellow actors they may well go home and do a proper job of learning them. The second type are the shy ones who are nervous of giving up their books for fear of being forgetful. They need a lot of coaxing and gentleness. If you have time, help them with their memorising on their own; or, if you are too rushed, ask the stage manager to help them.

Once the books have gone, you will be able to concentrate on what hands are doing and to watch out that props are being used accurately and convincingly. You will need to make decisions about which scenes need more rehearsal than others. There will always be the scenes which fall into place easily and those which never seem to go right. Sometimes a director can be tempted to leave out the easy scenes for too long so that they become the difficult ones when he or she has gone back to them.

There are no set rules about methods of rehearsal. Once the scenes are beginning to flow you will be considering the possibility of a run-through of the whole play. Invariably that first run-through will be disappointing; lines will be fluffed or forgotten; moves will get muddled and entrances will be made in the wrong places. This is inevitable and the wise director will not let the cast become dispirited. He or she will have made notes of the worst moments during the run-through and will hold special rehearsals to put them right.

Your rehearsals should keep a continuous balance between picking out the weak moments in scenes and the running of the scene itself, and between running the scenes individually and running the whole play. Without the run-throughs of scenes and the play you lose the flow of the action; without the specialised rehearsals, definition remains blurred.

Some rehearsals are best begun with a run-through of the play which will be followed up by working on the weak moments. At other times you will find it more helpful to concentrate on the weak moments first and end the rehearsal period with a run-through of the play. Or you can run through each scene and work on the weak moments as you progress through the play.

There are no rules. You will always need to accommodate your method of rehearsing to suit the needs of your particular cast, and be ready to think again if your method doesn't seem to be achieving the best results.

You will also need to judge just when to bring the rehearsals into the church. If you do this at too early a stage everyone may take fright, if you leave it too late there won't be time for making sure that everyone knows their way about the building and, most important of all, that the cast can be heard.

It's often helpful to move into the church a few weeks before the dress rehearsal. Your first rehearsals there will be taken up with adjusting to the building and to the acoustics. After this you might invite some outsider who knows nothing about the play to come to a rehearsal to see if they can hear from the back. The chances are you will all discover difficult moments in the play when the diction is not getting through. Don't leave this vital point till the dress rehearsal itself or you will produce a panic.

When thinking in terms of the dress rehearsal, don't expect to have only one. It's much more helpful to have a technical dress rehearsal before the full dress rehearsal. This enables the director to concentrate on the lighting, costumes, make-up, sound effects and the co-ordinating of 'house lights', and to concentrate on the acting during the second dress rehearsal.

A professional director knows that the company depend for their living on their work. Rehearsals will be maintained under strict discipline and the actor who is often absent could lose his job. But the director of an amateur company has to face the irritation caused by those members of the cast who feel (and not without reason), that their private lives are of more consequence than the play in which they are taking part ... 'I can't come to rehearsal tonight, because my husband has to have a tooth taken out', 'Please excuse me on Saturday, there's a family wedding', 'I have a headache', 'The plumber is coming', 'I just can't tear myself away from the TV'. The only course is to make as clear as possible *before rehearsals begin* that those taking part should dedicate themselves to the period of rehearsals and nothing short of an emergency should prevent them from attending. Give plenty of time to making clear to your company the absolute necessity of regular rehearsing. It is vital that the whole company should be available for every rehearsal. Of course they won't always be needed, but the director must be free to choose which scene to rehearse at any given time. As director try, as much as you can, to let your actors know in advance which scenes you are going to rehearse and when they will be needed.

'Mine is such a little part, just popping in and out of scenes and saying a few lines. I'm sure you won't need me this evening, will you?'

The answer may be 'No', but it is more likely to be 'Yes, we *do* need you'. The actor who is always 'popping in and out of scenes' needs a lot of rehearsing, both for his or her sake and for the sake of the rest of the company. Nothing looks more like a piece of patchwork than badly rehearsed small parts. The small part is far more significant than most people think it is. Years ago, during the war, Sir Laurence Olivier made an indelible impression on the British public by his performance as the Button Moulder in Ibsen's *Peer Gynt* at the New Theatre. His part was a tiny fraction of a long, rambling play; nevertheless, that performance remained in many minds long after some of the more important roles had been forgotten.

Never let your actors underestimate the value of their brief scenes. No one character is ever less important in a play than any other character. Think of the significance of the Porter in *Macbeth*. That scene is pivotal to the play, providing, as it does, a bridge between the deed and the consequence of the deed, it gives shape to the plot and a moment of relief from the insistent tension of the horror. The play grows more ominous because of that scene, and the part of the Porter sticks in the memory.

The performance of a play should look like a piece of woven cloth in which there should be no dropped stitches, no pieces of patchwork. And it is in this context that a director can give the small part players a sense of their place in the whole.

Above all, aim to keep your company together as a team. Don't allow those with leading roles to think of themselves as a cut above the others. Make sure that the company doesn't develop into cliques: dividing up into large-part players, small-part players, and the stage management. Encourage everyone concerned in the production to feel that they are a necessary part of the whole. Encourage the whole cast to feel involved even when they are sitting round in the rehearsal room waiting for their cue. Be very strict about 'no chattering' during rehearsal. Let everyone learn from everyone else and be interested in the others.

It's quite a helpful idea to provide moments during the production when grievances can be aired. They will be inevitable and it's healthy to air them but very unhealthy to allow them to be covered up and only whispered about in corners.

Christian companies are no less prone to this kind of furtive grumbling than non-Christian ones. But at least they can be reminded of the call to Christians to show love and tolerance towards their neighbours. Warn your company that they will not become immune from lack of charity towards each other simply because they are putting on a play in a church. It is often helpful to begin and end your rehearsals with a brief prayer. Let each member of the company take a turn in saying

the prayer. This will have a unifying effect on all concerned and become
a constant reminder of their trust in God's mercy.

'Yes, we *do* need to have all these rehearsals and it's a pity that we
can't manage to arrange more.' This should be the attitude of the
director of your play. Nothing less than the best we can offer should
be good enough for God. And, in the last resort, the play in church is
being offered to God; in joy, in praise, in compassion, in thanksgiving
for his marvellous creation.

The magic of
the spoken voice

However much has been done to ensure that your audience can see the actors in a church production, you will still have to make sure that they can be heard. Churches are noted for their difficult acoustics.

Most mediaeval churches were primarily designed for singing. Stone vaulting enhances the tone of the choir but it may add so many echoes to the spoken voice as to make it almost unintelligible. If you are careful enough in the choice of play for your church, you will take the acoustics very seriously into consideration. Before even choosing your play, consider the building where it will be acted. Take a friend with you and make some experiments with the sound. Stand in the acting area and shout at the top of your voice, 'Alleluia!' and wait for the echo to subside. If there is no appreciable echo, then go on to make further experiments to find how 'dead' the sound may be. Recite something unfamiliar or make up some inconsequential nonsense while your friend wanders round the building finding the good and bad places for understanding what you say. Then change roles: let him talk while you listen. And make sure you both listen from two-thirds back which is sometimes the worst part of the church for acoustics.

In some buildings – the 'dead' ones – you will have to fill your lungs, press with the diaphragm and raise your voice, if you are to be heard. In others – the over 'live' – words carry only if the voice is as flat as possible and the consonants are well articulated. A large audience, especially in the season of woolly clothing, will tend to soak up some of the volume and deaden echo.

In almost every case there will be some difficulties and all Groups who plan to act in churches should give special heed to the problem of voice production.

Whatever the play, certain rules apply to all church performances. The first is to concentrate on the consonants. Tongue, teeth and lips will have to work hard whether you are whispering your lines or shouting them. It is the t's and the d's, the p's and the b's, the l's and the r's, that will give your speech clarity, and they must be drawn round each word in a hard, sharp line.

In general, try to face forward and centre when speaking. Experiment will show you that in most churches lines delivered to the side are harder to distinguish. This is especially true at the crossing of a cruciform church. With your back to the audience, the problem is usually worse still, especially if there is a long chancel stretching behind you.

Another enemy of clarity is the tendency to drop the voice at the end of a sentence – 'I must tell you what happened to me last *Sunday*. We were sitting under the trees in the corner of the *park* when a man came along leading a *camel*.' What an extraordinary piece of information! But the *surprise* is taken out of it if all we hear is 'I must tell you what happened to me on ... We were sitting under the trees in the corner of the ... when a man came along leading a ...'

As director, you should watch very carefully to make sure that your cast speak as clearly as possible; as actor, you need to think all the time about the clarity of your voice. And watch out particularly for the last word in a line.

Being heard is essential, but there is more to the voice than simply being clear.

The human speaking voice is possibly the most varied and subtle musical instrument there is; and it is possibly the most neglected. Many people think of their voices in a fatalistic sort of way – 'that's the voice I was born with and I can't do anything about it' – as if they were talking about the shape of their noses or the size of their feet. Most of us forget how flexible our speaking voices are and what raw material they can be for producing marvellous results. What most of us are doing, in terms of musical notation, is to use about half an octave when we could be using a range of around two whole octaves.

It isn't the purpose of this book to write in detail about the use of the speaking voice, but simply to arouse an awareness in you, readers, as actors or directors, of the possibilities of what a voice can achieve, and to make a few suggestions.

Try speaking the following: *The tinkling of the glasses was followed by the booming of the guns.*

Listen to yourself, and repeat it. Did you make any distinction in tone between the two phrases? Did you read the passage more or less on one note? Then try again and this time colour what you are saying with something of the sound of the 'glasses' and the 'guns'. Now exaggerate the whole. Use the very highest notes in your voice for the first phrase and speak the second phrase on the lowest notes in your voice.

The tinkling of the glasses	*Using highest possible notes*
was followed by	*In your normal voice*
the booming of the guns	*Using lowest possible notes*

Of course this will sound completely over the top, but it is a useful exercise in stretching the range of your voice, and the idea can be adapted to other phrases.

Now speak these lines: *Whispering and murmuring the wind was breathing through the leaves.*

Did you listen to yourself? How much did your voice express the meaning of the words? Try again and let your voice adapt itself to the sounds in the sentence – the *whispering*, the *murmuring*, the *breathing*. Now exaggerate it. Once again it will be over the top, but the exercise will help your voice to be flexible.

Try saying aloud the following sentences, finding just the right kind of voice to express their meaning:

> The cold face stared
> Anger whipped into his eyes
> The star blazed
> Moonlight drifted over the snowy hill
> The thrumming of the drums
> The angels sang hallelujah

How did your voice sound? Did you allow each phrase its unique meaning? Or did they all sound very much the same? Go back to the phrases and make a picture of each one in turn. Then use your voice to express that picture. If necessary, repeat the same phrase several times till you are satisfied that your voice *is* expressing the picture. Gradually you find your voice stretching, that you can make it do things you never thought of before. Not only will you find yourself using more notes, but you will discover an ability to change the quality of your voice.

Sometimes it is helpful to think of your voice as if it were a box of paints. Just as a painter expresses the very quality of the trees, clouds, sunshine and flowers in his painting, so your voice can colour the lines it is speaking and make them come alive for others to see in their mind's eye.

Then, of course, there is the question of the rhythmic flow; and it's best to consider this in isolation at first. Here are a few simple exercises which can be used to develop a sense of rhythm:

> Up in the air the great bell swings
> Lifts up its clappers and down it rings

Try to capture the rhythm of the bell as you say the words.

> Pitter-patter on the window comes the spurt of rain

Keep to the insistent motion of the rain as you say this. Try repeating it over and over till you can hear the rain in your voice.

> Tick-tock
> tells the clock
> We'll be back
> by one o'clock

Turn your voice into the ticking of a clock for this. Make it sound mechanical.

> Softly the dove stirred in his hand
> Gently he held her there
> Then opened his fingers to set her free
> And smiled as she flew away into the air

Feel the movement of the bird and try to express it in your voice. Try, too, to capture the movement of the fingers and the bird flying away.

> March, march, march
> Up the hard road
> See the soldiers go
> Trudge, trudge, trudge

You could speak this one to the accompaniment of your own feet marching. Then stop marching and make your voice sound like your feet.

Your voice is an instrument, a musical instrument. And you need skill in playing on it. At this stage in becoming aware of the potential of your voice, begin to listen to other people. Note the range of voice used by members of your family. Listen to the announcers on the radio and television and observe the flexibility of their voices. How much would any of these be benefited by using an enlarged range of voice? How many of them appear to be managing with only half an octave? You will get some surprising results. Get into the habit of listening to voices in the shops, in buses, in the streets, at your place of work. Then start listening to your own voice. Of course this will make you extremely self-conscious for a while. As in acting you have to become self-conscious in order to lose self-consciousness.

Once your voice is becoming more flexible you could begin to think of other aspects of vocal range. There is the question of pace. A speech spoken at one level of speed can be monotonous. But break up the pace within the speech and people will find it easier to listen to you.

Let us take an imaginary speech from a play about Moses. Pharaoh's daughter is describing her discovery of the baby among the bulrushes:

> 1. I was just on my way to the waterside to have a bathe. 2. With me were Ira and Melita, my handmaids 3. when we heard a cry. 4. It wasn't like the crying of the riverbirds. 5. We listened and 6. held our breath. 7. Then we gathered up our skirts and ran. 8. We reached the edge of the river 9. and we stopped running 10. and listened again. 11. The cry was repeated, 12. but this time it was louder, and nearer. 13. Between me and Ira was a clump of bulrushes and the cry was coming from the clump. 14. I bent down and parted the rushes, 15. and there was a baby inside, 16. a baby boy!

If you read this speech all at the same pace you will miss the drama in it. But break up the pace like this and immediately it will come alive:

> 1. Moderate pace, unhurried
> 2. A little quicker
> 3. Very quick
> 4. A little slower
> 5. Slow
> 6. Quicker
> 7. Very quick
> 8. Slower
> 9. Slow
> 10. Very slow
> 11. Quicker
> 12. Very quick
> 13. Slower
> 14. Slow
> 15. Very quick
> 16. Very slow

As you try the speech in this way, note the effect of the variation of pace on the meaning of the piece. The character is remembering the event just as it happened and the change of pace represents the way in which each moment affected her. The last line, 'I bent down and parted the rushes' should be said slowly because there is a certain fear about what she is doing and she would not hurry it; 'and there

THE MAGIC OF THE SPOKEN VOICE 59

was a baby inside' is spoken very quickly because of the surprise and shock of discovery. This is followed by the very slow pace of the voice saying 'a baby boy' - to indicate the wonder of the discovery.

Let us imagine a speech which depends for its effectiveness on the gradual build up of pace, from slow to very quick.

Herod is ordering the massacre of the Innocents:

> **1.** Do not ask me to show mercy. **2.** Do not ask a king to show mercy to the enemy of his throne. **3.** When does an enemy show mercy? **4.** Does a ravaging lion let go its prey? **5.** Does thunder placate? **6.** Do as I tell you. **7.** Put the children to the sword.

Here we might pace it like this:

> **1.** Very slow
> **2.** Slow
> **3.** A little less slow
> **4.** A little quicker
> **5.** Quicker
> **6.** Quicker still
> **7.** Very quick

The man is building up his own argument, is persuading himself as much as he is persuading those about him. The pace has to keep mounting in order to convince him that what he is doing is justified. In the end the decision comes with a rush. He speaks the last words, 'Put the children to the sword!' very fast to forestall any second thoughts.

At this stage in your awareness of the potential in your voice, you might begin to adapt what you are learning to your own lines in the play. If you are the director, you will begin to think about all these aspects of the voice and work on the speeches your actors are learning in the light of what you are discovering about their voices.

We have considered change of note, of the use of tone, of the development of a sense of rhythm and control of pace. We haven't, as yet, thought about one very simple aspect of the voice which is piano and forte (soft and loud) which ranges from pianissimo - very soft - to fortissimo - very loud. It is possible to speak in a whisper and be heard just as clearly as if you were shouting. So long as consonants are sharp and clear the voice is being projected (thrown forward and not muffled); there is no reason why the range of soft and loud used in a church should not be a wide one. Remember that anything which gives variation to the voice helps to keep the interest of your audience. A monotonous voice is soporific, a varied voice attracts attention.

A useful exercise to practise vocal crescendo and diminuendo is to repeat these lines spoken by a night watchman in years gone by:

> Past ten o'clock and a fine bright night.

Pretend that you are standing backstage and wanting to achieve the effect of the watchman arriving from a distance, drawing nearer and nearer till he is level with the acting area before going off into the distance again, his call becoming fainter and fainter as the sound disappears altogether. Try speaking the line on one note only (no subtlety of tone or expression for the watchman who has to be heard clearly by everyone in the village) and to use no other variation in your voice than that of volume. Try saying it seven times to begin with, letting the fourth call become the one level with the acting area and therefore the loudest. As you get better at controlling the volume (and it isn't as easy as it looks!), try increasing the number of your calls – the more calls you can make, the greater the range of volume in your voice.

It is a temptation to use loud and soft notes without much subtlety. Simply to speak loudly when a character is angry will not become a substitute for real anger which can often be quiet and icy cold. Soft notes are not always the best way to express wonder or tenderness. Look out for the true meaning behind what the character in the play is saying and use your range of volume to underline that meaning. Search your speeches for internal change of volume; for instance, a Rabbi is complaining:

> 1. This man, Jesus, has corrupted the people. 2. He gives them free bread in order to win their admiration. 3. He has healed on the Sabbath Day!

At a glance it might seem that the best way to express the man's anger would be to use full volume. But try taking 1. with deliberation, at a moderate volume; 2. louder as the man's indignation becomes aroused; 3. with very little volume indeed but with an icy and a bitter emphasis.

You may, by now, feel inclined to buy a book on the use of the voice and there are many *good ones* available. You might consider taking lessons. Both could be of advantage so long as you make this study a servant and not a master. You can only hope to develop the potential of your voice little by little and it can be a lifetime's study. So while you are in the process, never let your attention depart from the meaning of what you are saying. Your voice is there to interpret the meaning, not to show off its newly-discovered range.

There are many ways in which the human voice can be used to create an almost musical effect which can be especially effective in church drama. When more than one voice speaks at a time you get a sense of an added dimension. The Greeks understood this in their use of the Chorus. So did T. S. Eliot with his Women of Canterbury in *Murder in the Cathedral*. These choruses coming, as they do, between powerfully dramatic scenes, and commenting on them, provide the play with what amounts to musical interludes much in the manner of the sung chorus in a musical, which lifts the story and moves it on. You can use choral speaking when dramatising passages from the Bible and in the voice dramas as mentioned in Chapter Four. Choral speaking can enhance scenes in plays, can colour them and provide a verbal backdrop against which your main characters will stand out more vividly.

But however beautiful the musical effect may be, no director should become so entranced by the result as to allow the music of the words to overlie the meaning of the words.

Nothing will happen overnight. Don't be discouraged if you can't achieve remarkable changes quickly. As actor or director, recognise the potential and work towards achieving it. Remember the speaking voice is an instrument which is a servant of the word, and thank God for it.

Getting into character

There is a tendency in the theatre to divide parts up into 'straight' and 'character'. As a result those playing 'straight' parts may feel that there is little to be done except to interpret the part as an offshoot of their own personality, whereas the 'character' part players tend to put on their characters like so many comic hats.

In all acting there is always an element of both 'straight' and 'character'. No one person is ever the same as any other one person. However close to you in personality your part may be, that part will never be *you*. However much your part is at variance from you there will always be a germ of *you* inside it. Every part that every actor plays is at one and the same time both 'straight' and 'character'.

As the first thing to be done when a play is being rehearsed is to read it, your first consideration both as actor or director will be to think about the voice of your character. If your part has a decided regional accent make sure, as actor, that you manage it convincingly. Don't resort to Mummerset or the equivalent. Get good records or cassette tapes from the BBC or British Theatre Association and study these. If you know anyone with the accent you are wanting to imitate, ask them to make a recording of your part. This will be more help than anything. As director, be prepared to alter an accent to suit your actors if necessary. It's better to give up an accent altogether than to get it wrong. But if your actors have settled on learning unfamiliar accents, suggest that they learn their parts *with* the accents, rather than memorise them first and fit in the accent afterwards.

In some cases the playwright doesn't define the accents to be used by his characters, though it may seem clear from the text that certain regional accents would be called for. In this case it's important to discuss this with your cast before you begin the first reading of the play. For instance the shepherds in a Nativity play would certainly have country accents, but they must have the same one, otherwise they will appear to be a very mixed bunch!

Once again comes the need to listen to others. Cultivate the habit of listening to the voices around you, on buses, in the street, in shops, at home, at school, in the office, in the factory. You will be surprised by their variety. Television and radio give us excellent opportunities for listening to the voices we shan't often be hearing in our own locality. All actors and directors should become good listeners.

The voice of a character isn't only influenced by the part of the world he comes from or the society he mixes with. Age plays a large part in determining the kind of voice anyone uses. Children's voices are usually high and loud. Have you ever listened to children in a playground? The older people get, the less certain their voices often become and usually the pitch drops. Voices are an expression of our complete personality, otherwise how would we be able to recognise our friends on the telephone? The use of inflection can play a vital part in creating the mood of a character. Upward inflections suggest a person's positive qualities, while the depressed or miserable tend to use downward inflections. Authoritative people are often marked by the lack of any inflection at all. Once again the need is to listen. How do the voices of your friends indicate their moods? What voices characterise your family? Your boss? Your girlfriends? Your boyfriends? Listen for their inflections and make mental notes of them. And don't forget to listen to your fellow actors. But don't copy their inflections otherwise the scene between you and them will be flat and boring.

We now have to think about the kind of bodies our characters possess. Are they old, young, fat, thin, in pain, vigorous, crippled, lethargic, graceful? Your character's body is something that needs to be 'put on' at the earliest stage of rehearsal. Of course this will take time and should never be rushed. We have to feel our way into the bodies of our characters rather than put them on like coats, and in order to fit yourself into the body of your character you will need to neutralise your own body to give it a different shape and nature and fill it with the body of another person. Of course this metamorphosis can only take place in the imagination (except in those occasional instances where you may find yourself wearing padding for a fat body), and you will need to practise the ability to 'picture' yourself into the body of someone else. All too often inexperienced actors tend to wait till they are into costume before they think themselves into the body of their character hoping that the costume will affect the necessary change. If your actors haven't created the bodies of their parts well before the dress rehearsal, their costumes, far from helping the character to emerge, will look out of place. Have you ever watched inexperienced actors wearing Roman togas over their twentieth-century bodies? The result is to make them look as if they were wearing fancy dress. The efficient actor can almost make you believe he is wearing period costume when he is actually rehearsing in practice dress because his imagination has been giving him another body.

And then, of course, these bodies have to make gestures and to move about. The arms of an actor are not a pair of signalling devices to be lifted up and down because of a director's note. All gesture springs from the body and at no time should the arms look as if they were independent of the main trunk of the character. 'Lo, there is a star!' should not be accompanied by the mere lifting of an arm, but by the whole person of the actor aware of the beautiful light in the sky to which the arm is pointing. The raised, clenched fist in 'Crucify him!' should spring from a tension of hatred within the depths of the actor. Similarly, the hands held out in greeting when the Prodigal Son's father is welcoming him home should not look like a couple of semaphore flags, but should be the outcome of the very heart of warmth and thankfulness within the character.

Arms and hands are never isolated from the body. They are always at work expressing what a person is feeling. Notice how people pick at their fingers when they are nervous, how hands can be rubbed together in anticipation of good news, how palms touch each other in thought. Once again, watch out for these hand movements in others and use what you have observed when creating your character. 'I don't know what to do with my hands' is often the cry of the actor who is learning his craft. It's all too easy for the director to say, 'Don't think about them', and the actor replies, 'I think about nothing else, they're so embarrassing.' The hands will remain embarrassing so long as the actor feels them to be two flags at the end of two poles. But the moment those hands come to be at the receiving end of the inmost feelings of the character portrayed by the actor, they will cease to be an embarrassment, and will become vital indicators of emotion.

The same applies to movement. Never let your imagination stop working on the body of your character either in motion or repose. Suppose you are playing the part of a nervous, tentative person; let every movement be charged with hesitancy. A nervous person may glance at a chair before sitting down to make sure it's still there; their feet will reflect the uncertainty of their nature and will tend to tread only on the balls and toes for fear of seeming too downright; they may have a fear of falling or of being pushed over which will make them look around them as they walk; their hands may move uncertainly between one gesture and another to indicate apprehension at making any kind of a decision.

But suppose your character is a bossy, self-assured type; keep the trunk of your body upright and the shoulders well back; walk firmly and decisively so that the whole of the foot is pressing into the ground; you know where the chair is and don't have to glance round before you sit down; you may keep your hands almost clenched to indicate your grasp of any situation.

Practise walking and sitting in the body of your character at home. Get familiar with the physical feel of being inside that person, whether nervous, self-assured, depressed, ebullient, hysterical, calm – the list is endless – till you can bring it to rehearsal without undue self-consciousness. It will become almost second nature to you after a time.

Possibly the most difficult kind of part to play is that of the natural character, the man or woman who is open to life and isn't plagued by inhibitions or hang-ups. Imagine playing the part of St John or the young David of the Old Testament; or, for a woman, that of the young Mary, or, in the Old Testament, Ruth or Rebecca. You want to give the impression of easy, natural people who move without nervousness or aggression, whose walk is liberated because their souls are free, and whose hands are open and relaxed to indicate generous natures. For such parts the first essential is relaxation. Try swinging your arms loosely from the shoulders, letting the hands fall freely (this isn't as simple as it looks). Ask a friend to lift your arm and then let it fall. If the arm falls loosely you have relaxed it. If not, then you will need to do some more swinging till you can achieve that complete letting go of will and muscle. Practise walking easily in bare feet with steps that are at the same time firm and light. Practise sitting down with ease and grace, on a stool, a chair or even the floor. Such characters convey the openness and spontaneity of their natures by the flow of their movements and their natural ability to feel at ease.

Certain emotions produce tension in the body and its movement. Fear and anger are conveyed through the muscles and are expressed through a tautening of limbs, Fear can produce a sickening feeling in the stomach; anger can make the whole body tremble. Recall moments when you, yourself, were affected by these emotions and use what you can remember of their effect on your body to reproduce the same effect in your character.

The converse is true of joy. All too often we find joy being expressed only by the voices of actors. Their tongues are shouting 'Hallelujah!' while their bodies are inert and the legs slightly bent. Joy, like any other emotion, permeates the entire corpus, giving the muscles an illusion that they are made of light. In moments of great exultation we feel we could take wing and fly. Lightness pervades our whole being and the instinct is to walk with a spring, or to want to dance.

Legs, like hands, are barometers of emotion. Straight, upright legs indicate positive feelings of power, joy, hope and fervour, while sagging, bent legs show us the inner uncertainty, depression or sense of inferiority expressed by their owner. Legs are indicative, too, of age and health. Remember how the old are often crippled by pain in their legs, how the prosperous middle-aged are firmly fixed on theirs, whereas the young are able to move as if their legs were on springs.

Gestures, like body movement, should always be significant. Too many gestures may indicate that the actor has put them in without considering exactly *why* the character is making them. A gesture should always supply a clue to the character in any given scene. Gestures such as: fidgeting with a pair of spectacles, tapping a table with the fingers, fussing with hair, tapping with the feet, stroking the chin, knocking knuckles together, can all indicate the nature and mood of a character. But they should be used sparingly. Too many gestures can become fussy and restless (unless the actor is playing a fussy and restless part), and the general effect can become blurred.

Conversely, stillness can be enormously powerful and both actors and director should be on the look-out for those moments in a scene when everyone is still. Actors should try to cultivate a quality of stillness when they are not actually moving. This is more difficult than it seems. The actor who has not had much experience finds it harder to be still when he is neither moving nor talking than anything else. He is inclined to fill in that space with minute, meaningless shifts of position.

But whether actors are gesturing, moving or simply staying still, it is vital that they should know why their characters are so doing, and the director should help the cast by working out these details with them. The actor needs to relate each move or gesture given to him or her by the director to the truth about the character he or she is interpreting and if this seems too difficult the director should be turned to for further help in making it all clear. Nothing becomes less convincing than performances given in a kind of no-man's-land between the convictions held by actor and director. Somehow or other the same truth must be perceived by both of them.

These ideas belong as much to the playing of small parts or being part of a chorus as they do to the creation of a leading character. Even if you are only a part of a crowd, remember how important your part is. If only one member of a chorus fails to keep the imagination alight and lapses into some kind of native droopiness, the tension in the scene immediately drops. A play is like a painting, the smallest detail is significant, take it away, and there is a hole in the picture. No one in the play is ever without significance. A crowd in which each member has realised some particular character and is letting the imagination create the body of that character will be quite startling in its realism, and will give a much-needed support to the leading actors.

Actors are interdependent, usually working as part of a group.

The character portrayed is never isolated from any other character in the play. The ability to listen to what your fellow actors are saying is a vital part of establishing the truth of your own character. In real life we don't know what our friend is going to say and so we listen for it. Too often actors, who *do* know in one sense what their fellow actors are going to say, should remember to listen as if they had no idea of what is about to be said.

Such listening isn't only done with the ear, waiting for the cue line and then pouncing in with one's own bit. It means also listening to the nature of the characters sharing the scene with us, watching for the signals - signs of nervousness, the glint of power, eyes growing tender or hard - which warn or encourage our character. Remember everything in the play is happening for the first time. It is all happening *now*. This is the keynote to freshness and realism. And it involves this special type of listening.

Suppose our play is about the Passion. The Disciples don't know whether or not Jesus is to be crucified till it happens. The characters round the Cross don't know that Jesus will rise on the third day. When the two Marys go to the tomb on that Sunday morning, they don't expect to find it empty; when the Angel speaks to them they don't know who he is.

Getting into character means also being intensely aware of the other characters. Not as Maud or Betty or Dick or Harry playing their parts, but as Mary and Mary Magdalene, the Centurion and the Apostle John. The need is to perceive the truth about every character in the play because in a play everyone is a part of everyone else. Whether the part is small or large makes no difference. All parts are equally important to the success of the whole.

There will often occur moments in religious plays when the miraculous happens and it will be difficult for many actors who haven't experienced any such kind of supernatural occurrence to make it seem real. Take, for instance, the arrival of the angels in the fields of Bethlehem. How are your actors going to portray angels? How are the shepherds to react?

Perhaps the most helpful way in which an actor can connect the supernatural vision to his own experience is by recalling the most startling, vivid and beautiful experience of his own life. It may have been the sun setting between mountains; it may have taken place when he looked into the face of someone and knew for the first time that he loved them; or a childhood memory of the sea at high tide; a poem, or a piece of music. There will be as many different moments of vision as there are actors to recollect them. But use these recollections that are unique to one person only to make real that vision in the play.

Alas, it is all too easy to let these supernatural moments become sentimental when in fact they can be shattering and not without a tinge of fear. The angels in the Bible came with warnings as well as greetings. Mary was frightened, at first; so were the shepherds; so must Joseph have been when he was told to escape into Egypt. These angels are not the little figures we buy over the counter at Christmas with paper wings and gilded hair. They are presences from the thundering majesty of the Kingdom of God. Never portray an angel glibly. Wafting about in a long white robe will not be good enough. You must imagine that you are alight with the Holy Spirit. Feel as if your body were made of flames, as if your eyes were coals of fire, and you may give your audience some impression of what Mary, the shepherds and Joseph saw.

'You have spoken about the voice, about the body, arms and legs of a character, but what about the face?' You, the reader, may well be asking this. Faces are the most obvious keys to character and some less experienced actors can be trapped into feeling that facial expression is something external, like a mask which can be put on and taken off at will. Of course the face is the most expressive feature we have, but its expressiveness must never be put on. It must grow from within. The more you have thought about the physical aspect of the character, the more real his or her body has become, the more naturally will your face express that character's nature and feelings.

Acting is not about making faces. It is not about putting on a mask. Acting is concerned with thinking and feeling yourself so deeply into your part that the face will naturally express the character.

Some actors rehearse by watching themselves in the looking-glass. This is often a dangerous trick which can lead the actor to thinking too much of what he is looking like and inhibit him from forgetting himself and letting the part take over.

Perhaps we shouldn't think in terms of 'putting on', but of allowing oneself to be 'invaded by' another character. And this can't be done overnight. All the moves, all the voice control, all the correct handling of props will never take the place of that sympathetic and creative imagining which will be ultimately reflected in facial expression. The Duchess says to Alice, in Wonderland, 'Take care of the sense and the sounds will take care of themselves.' The actor might well paraphrase it as 'Take care of the thoughts and the face will take care of itself.'

Acting is about truth and about sympathy. Techniques of 'getting into character' are necessary, but ultimately it is the truth about a character which makes him 'tick', and it is this truth which the Christian actor will always be seeking.

Characters in plays are, to some extent, our neighbours. Most authors base their characters on people they have known. To what extent, then, is the actor 'loving his neighbour' when he is taking on a role? We will be thinking about this profound question in the next chapter.

ELEVEN

Acting — A form of
loving one's neighbour

It is not uncommon for someone to say to a professional actor, 'Of course I never know whether you mean what you say because you are an actor.' The implication here is that actors spend their time displaying false feelings and are not to be trusted. But really, the opposite is true. Actors have to learn to use real feelings and channel them into the roles they are playing. If their feelings are false they will become what is known as 'ham' actors and what they say and do on stage will not move the audience either to laughter or to tears.

As we have said before, the theatre is about truth. Far from covering your feelings, as an actor you are called upon to learn to express them, which may have the result that you find it more difficult to conceal them. Of course, all the feelings that you are called upon to display cannot possibly be ones that you have experienced yourself. But you should try to use your imagination to get as close as you can to those emotions which may be alien to you. And it is in this attempt to discover the truth about other people's hearts that you are given a unique opportunity to love your neighbour.

How do actors find out about feelings that are not theirs? It isn't easy to play the part of a murderer if you have never even wanted to hit someone. So how would you play the part of Cain? How would you play Mary Magdalene? These are extreme examples and we will go back to them. Let us think first of what it would be like to play the part of someone totally different from ourselves.

The very first essential for an actor is the quality of sympathy, which means 'feeling with'. If, on the whole, you are someone who genuinely loves people and are not condemnatory of them, the chances are that you have the makings of an actor. If you can laugh with them and cry with them, then you are the sort of person who can begin to take part in the making of a play.

In the last chapter we thought about the physical attributes necessary to create a character and of how all these attributes have to be prompted from within. Now we are thinking about that quality which is *within*. It seems sometimes to be locked up in a person like a treasure in a cupboard. How do we find the key?

Perhaps the most helpful beginning to a search for the 'withinness' of a character is to study their background. Suppose your part is that of Brenda, a poor woman surrounded by screaming children who is at her wits' end. You have a regular job in an office and go back each evening to a quiet bed-sitting-room. How do you imagine that woman's life? First of all look round to see which of your friends might fit most closely into Brenda's life. Perhaps there is Dorothy, an old school contemporary with three children and an invalid husband. It's true you haven't seen Dorothy blow her top. But weren't you aware the last time you had lunch with her of how thin she had grown and how tired she looked? Remember she had developed a habit of picking at her fingers, and biting her lips when one of the children spilled their orange juice or milk. You came away really worried about her. Try walking in the park at the weekends and studying other mothers with their families. Or in the supermarket. Gradually you may find just the right way to interpret your part of Brenda. And you will have learned something more valuable, a greater sympathy for Dorothy and for all the other Dorothys in the world.

Perhaps you have been cast for the part of Douglas who is out of work and given to fits of melancholy. You yourself are active and cheerful. You have a good job in a bank and are happily married. Maybe you have a friend, Tom, who is also out of work. He lives with his parents and although he never grumbles when you visit him, his parents tell you how worried they are about his depressions. This may give you an opportunity of helping Tom to open up. You tell him about the part of Douglas and ask his advice. Tom will probably tell you a lot about himself and his melancholy that he has never told anyone before. You will have learned a lot about Douglas but, more important, you will have helped Tom.

Suppose you are called upon to play the part of St Peter? There aren't many saints around on your visiting list. Though, wait a minute, what about that uncle of yours who gives his life to the care of disabled children? There's nothing very 'holy' about Uncle Steve, yet you often hear people describe him as a saint. As far as you can remember he has enjoyed his work with the children; at least you have never heard him moan about it. But he's quite ordinary. There's nothing in his rather scruffy appearance to suggest he is special. Except, perhaps, for his cheerfulness. He enjoys his pipe and likes his pint at the local on evenings off. So how does this relate to St Peter? How is *your* sympathy to relate to the part? You will probably find yourself distancing yourself from it with the thought, 'I could never play a saint like him', forgetting that saints are not animated statues, but real people who walked and ate and slept and washed just like the rest of us. So think of the humanity of Peter. Concentrate on the practical fisherman with the roughened hands and the far-seeing eyes. Go and spend a day with Uncle Steve (if he will let you) and watch how he handles the broken bodies of those children with such care and such expertise at the same time making light of it all and telling them funny stories. You will learn a lot about your part and be the richer person for it. And you will have gained a new love and respect for that scruffy uncle.

When you are playing the part of someone in a bygone age, you will also need to imagine the physical life of that period which may be very different from the twentieth century. Get some history books and read about the kind of dwellings people lived in; did they have roads? what sort of food would they have eaten? how were they governed?

Acting is about real people. St Peter isn't just a draped figure from the pictures in your Bible. Historical characters were as alive in their time as you are now. Brenda and Douglas are not fictions springing from the mind of the playwright. They are all as real as the crowds in the street, as the members of your family.

Some people talk as if acting were only a form of 'showing-off'. Of course that may be a part of the picture. We all like to 'show off'. Even ministers of religion taking the 'lead' parts in services do, to some extent, 'show off'. So do teachers and doctors, salesmen and lawyers. Most people achieve some means for 'showing-off', even if it takes the form of ostentatiously *not* 'showing-off'. We all like our identity to be established. Of course actors like to 'show-off'. But if they are going to be of any value at all in their performance, they must also be committed to an activity which is akin to Jesus' command to 'love thy neighbour as thyself'.

It may appear strange that there could be a connection between loving one's neighbour and acting. It certainly isn't a link that is often remarked on. And yet it is there. In putting on the coat or hat of my friend, I become, superficially, a little like my friend. But in assuming the character and personality of another person, I am, in a deeper sense, taking on their very nature.

Dame Sybil Thorndike, that great Christian actress, used to say that there were certain characters she didn't look forward to portraying because they were unpleasant and alien to her. But, she said, after she had been rehearsing them for some weeks she found, to her humbling amazement, those very unpleasantnesses hidden away in her own nature.

Such experiences of self-discovery can lead actors to a greater understanding of their fellow men, can help them to become more tolerant, more forgiving. 'To know all is to understand all' becomes real for actors who have taken on unsympathetic roles. This is not to be mistaken for actors taking on the sins of their characters and condoning them. Rather they discover what has led to the committing of sins. They don't condone, any more than they would condone their own weaknesses. But, in understanding, they are accepting the sinful, weak characters as fellow human beings. They are no longer standing outside and judging.

Acting is concerned with true sympathy. How many of us, in our constant struggle to be more loving, can have this unique opportunity of getting inside a fellow human being?

How often do we struggle to be kind to that tiresome old woman who talks all day about her rheumatism? To have patience with the irritating health fanatic who boasts about his twenty-mile jog before breakfast? To tolerate the teenager who systematically tears our treasured concepts into shreds? It is often easier to love out-and-out sinners than to bear with those we find exasperating. But meet people in a comedy, in the part you may be playing yourself, and you discover what it is like to experience pain every time you get up from a chair; what it costs, in terms of self denial, to run those twenty miles before breakfast; how hard it is to be brimful of ideas which the middle-aged don't want to hear about. You will also find, in the comedy, that these characters are funny. You can laugh with them as well as at them. And this is how you may begin to love them.

So what happens when your part is Cain, or Mary of Magdala before her life was changed? Perhaps we can concentrate our imaginations best on the motives which drive people to kill or to sell their bodies. The jealousy and the desperation which we all feel at times is merely magnified in them.

There are so many different kinds of people and we know so little about one another. Are you poor, and have a dislike of the affluent? Try playing the part of a rich man obsessed with his possessions, lonely in the middle of his grandeur, and you will cease to condemn him. Are you rich and indifferent to the plight of the poor? Then perhaps you may have the privilege of playing the part of the beggar at the gate of Lazarus and understand, from inside, what it is like to be hungry and dirty and to have no money in the bank.

Are you as fit as a fiddle? See what happens when you take on the role of someone who is sick. Self-assured? You will be surprised when you play a terrorised vacillator. Are you too timid and self-effacing to speak your mind at church meetings? You will be astonished by the change in your attitude after you have played the part of a dominating politician.

We have been thinking of 'opposites'. But not all acting is as different from our own personalities. Very often we find ourselves 'type-cast'. In this case, whatever you do, don't sit back and think you can walk about the stage with your own self, using your own voice and moving with the rhythms of your own body. As we said in the previous chapter, whatever part you take on will not be *you*. Even an identical twin has a totally different personality from the other twin. We are all as unique as our finger-prints.

It is always helpful, in cases of so-called 'type-casting', to look first for the differences between the actor's and the character's personality and nature. Pin-point those differences, understand and sympathise with them, and use them to establish the character in all its uniqueness. Rejoice in the differences. They are all a part of God's creation. And in this understanding and sympathy with the differences between you and your character will come a new understanding and sympathy for those around you, your friends, your family and your neighbours.

Have you ever used a glove-stretcher? You take the limp, washed glove, with the fingers looking rather like withered twigs, put the stretcher into each finger, one by one, and suddenly you have the filled-out shape of a human hand. This is what happens to the actor. He gets stretched as a human being. He becomes filled out with new insights and experiences. He has embraced the character of a neighbour and has learned to love him.

Christianity is concerned with loving our neighbour, and theatre is about that, too. The neighbours can be tiresome, malicious, ridiculous, wicked, as well as heroic and good; but our job, as actors, is to be in sympathy with them, to feel with them and to discover what makes them tick.

So when someone asks why you are taking part in a play in a church and what drama can have to do with religion, you will be able to reply; 'A play is about my neighbours and is helping me to love them.'

Backstage community

In the professional theatre a great many people are employed backstage –
in fact they often outnumber the actors by two to one – but this is not
usually the case with amateurs. One reason may be that the work seems
a good deal less glamorous than acting. Another is almost certainly
that most amateurs have far less time and money to spend on the
technical side, and for productions in church this is probably just as
well. If you are going to make use of the natural advantages offered to
you by the building, then it is a mistake to try and disguise it as a theatre
or to dazzle the audience with too many effects.

Nevertheless, you would be very unwise to try and manage without
some kind of stage crew, however simple and uncluttered your show.
Above all, you will definitely need a STAGE MANAGER, the person
responsible for running the actual performance; making contact with
the front-of-house to know if the audience has arrived; saying when the
show is to begin; seeing that everything is in place beforehand, that the
lighting and sound effects come in when required, that the actors have
all their costumes and properties. These are not really suitable duties
for the director, especially on the first night. They need somebody with
a cool head, who is not worrying about whether people will like the
show. It is not the stage manager's job to decide whether So-and-So is
giving a good performance, only to make sure that So-and-So is dressed
correctly, carrying the stick or whatever and coming on at the right
moment in the right place.

For this reason the stage manager needs to be present from the very
first rehearsal, and a wise director will have had several conferences
with him or her even before then. When the moves are being plotted,
the stage manager should be sitting at a table, writing every one of them
into a script, which is known as the PROMPT COPY, and noting
every change in subsequent rehearsals. When the script demands that
the Shepherd should come in carrying a lamb, the stage manager makes
a note that a lamb is needed. If that doesn't seem possible, the director
must be told at the earliest opportunity.

If the director wants the audience to see somebody crucified before
their eyes, then it is the stage manager who will have to work out how

it is to be done or otherwise protest in good time. Naturally, decisions of this kind should have been taken long in advance, but practical problems will keep coming up all the way through rehearsals, and the stage manager is there to solve them. When you are gathering your team, choose your stage manager with as much care as your leading performers; he or she can be the greatest possible asset to you.

Independent of, but preferably working very closely with, the stage manager is the DESIGNER, who is responsible for how the show will look. Strictly speaking, this job is not part of the stage staff, because the design work should be over by the dress rehearsal. How much there is to do will depend very much on the show and on your style of production. Are you making costumes specially? Then the designer will have to produce the designs and will usually buy the materials. Are you hiring them? Leave the designer to choose. Are the actors dressing themselves? Then everything they plan to wear must be seen and approved by the designer. The same applies to every item of scenery and properties; the designer must design, choose or at least approve them all. Because this work is over so early, the job of designer can be combined with another if necessary. Sometimes the director will do it, sometimes the stage manager, sometimes one of the performers. The important thing is to recognise that it must be done by somebody. Far too many amateur productions are presented with no design at all.

If you are using any quantity of music, you will need a MUSICAL DIRECTOR, whose relations with the director may vary a great deal from show to show. They may, of course, be one and the same person. If not, then the director will have to take careful heed of everything the musical director says, especially in a full-scale musical, but in the last analysis the director must always remain in charge. If you yourself are not very musical, then you would almost certainly be unwise to direct a musical show unless you have a musical director who is prepared to be extremely co-operative with you. Plenty of productions are ruined by the musical director insisting on standing the singers in impossible places or making a total sacrifice of the sense to the sound. On the other hand, a good musical director who really wants to help can almost lift your show up to the skies.

If you are designing costumes for the production, then naturally you will need one or more WARDROBE ASSISTANTS to make them up. Even if you are hiring them or simply asking the actors to wear their own clothes, you would still be wise to have someone with a needle standing by. It is wardrobe's job to cut and stitch the materials, turning the designer's sketches into reality and making sure that they are comfortable and practicable for the actors to wear. When something rips, wardrobe should mend it, and (in theory at least) they are responsible for washing the costumes, though in most amateur companies the performers do their own. The wardrobe master or mistress has a double responsibility – to the designer, for following the designs (or objecting when they are impossible), and to the stage manager for producing the costumes on time. In return, they must protect the wardrobe staff from the actors: 'I say, do you think you could make these breeches a bit tighter? I look as if I'm wearing plus-fours'; 'Would you come and be my dresser for Scene Three? I'll never make the change otherwise'; 'Would it be an awful nuisance, while you're washing those costumes, to slip in my dress shirt?' The first question should have gone to the designer, the second to the stage manager, and the third should never have been asked at all.

You may very well need a STAGE CARPENTER, especially if you want to build a stage for the church, but also for other less ambitious jobs as well. For instance, you may want a full-sized Cross, or a rostrum for Pilate's chair to stand on or some kind of constructional scenery. Remember that a carpenter is exercising a difficult skill and may know a good deal more about what is possible than either the director or the designer.

If your play is being performed at night, you will almost certainly have to have an ELECTRICIAN, even if only to turn the church lights off and on, but with the right equipment he can do a great deal more than that. Lighting, even in its simplest and crudest form, is a vital part of design, and, at its best, it can create a world of magic. In the theatre, of course, there is normally a vast electrical installation, whereas the average church may have a very dicey power supply indeed. In fact, the first thing the electrician needs to know is where to find the fuse box, so it is important to choose somebody who is trusted by the church authorities.

Both the electrician and the carpenter are likely to know a lot more about their craft than you do, so they can help you a great deal, if only you will let them. Listen to what they have to say with great respect, but remember that they cannot release you from the responsibility of making the decisions.

You may also wish to use recorded sound. Like the electrician, the SOUND OPERATOR will need somewhere inconspicuous to hide with all the equipment, in a place where it is easy to follow the play and take cues from the stage manager. It is a curious fact that, whereas very few people would offer to act as carpenter or electrician, a great number fancy they are quite competent to run the sound. The most important thing is to make sure that they understand the equipment and can make it do what they want. Most sound operators are safest using their own.

Of course, the stage manager may combine one or more of these jobs, but in a big production there may be far too much to do already. Over and above the primary job of sitting in at every rehearsal, making notes in the script and prompting when required, there may be other things crying out to be done. The carpenter wants to pin the apron stage to the pulpit, which will mean catching the Vicar and smoothing down the verger as well. The local school have offered to lend some lighting, and someone has got to collect it this evening in a car. One of the sidesmen had a beautiful velvet jacket at the last Harvest Supper, and now's the moment for asking him to lend it: 'It's quite safe – it'll only be worn for a couple of minutes at the end of the play, and wardrobe have promised to wrap it in tissue paper the moment it comes offstage.'

All told, we look like having a busy evening. We can't be at rehearsal, but we must know what's happening, because they're doing Scene Three again, and the director keeps changing the moves. There is nothing else for it – we must have an ASSISTANT STAGE MANAGER. That ASM is soon going to be indispensable. The stage can't be put up until two days before the show, but the ASM can mark out the area every night with bright electrician's tape, and clear it up again afterwards so that nobody can tell we've been there. Then there's prompting, altering moves in the book, making or finding small props and running endless messages, even making coffee for everyone during rehearsals. In the professional theatre, the assistant stage manager is usually a job for the young, who are expected to make themselves useful in any way they can.

These are the main categories of stage staff, but of course the number may easily increase because of all the assistants that are needed. The carpenter may need one or more assistants if there are really a stage and scenery to be built. With a complicated lighting plot, the electrician may not have enough hands to manage alone. We have already assumed there may be more than one person on wardrobe. Conversely, the numbers can shrink if the load is not too heavy. The electrician doubles the job of sound operator, the stage manager is also the carpenter, and the designer takes over the wardrobe.

In certain, very simple, church productions, the stage staff may wither away altogether. If you are putting on a ten-minute sketch instead of a sermon, you will not want to be bothered with the great crowd of people listed above. You might just run to a stage manager, but more probably you will have nobody at all. But, just because you are not using the people, does not mean that you can get out of doing the work. Someone has got to make sure that the furniture and properties are there, that the actors are wearing the right clothes and know when to begin. Somebody has to check that the necessary doors are unlocked and the right lights switched off and on. Untold productions have been held up because a well-meaning busybody has locked a vital door or worked a two-way switch at the back of the church.

However many they are or few, the most important thing about the backstage staff is that they should work together harmoniously with one another and with the cast. The responsibility for this lies with the stage manager, who should infuse a sense of joy and purpose into the group, so that they act as a unified team. Much of the secret of this lies in making them realise that the production belongs to them just as much as to the actors. There is great satisfaction in the smooth running of the show, all the cues following one another like clockwork, the costumes well executed and the properties safely in place. All this aspect of the play should be like a feat of apparently effortless engineering, and the hallmark of real success is that the audience should never notice it.

It is not only a question of the stage staff getting on with one another. One of the greatest dangers for any drama group is tension between the stage staff and the performers. It is easy enough to understand. Up till the dress rehearsal, the actors have been straining their hearts and imaginations in the attempt to do what the director wants. Now suddenly what seemed like a work of art has become more like battledrill in hostile country. Instead of the director, it is the stage manager who is ordering them about, with no apparent interest in the quality of their performance but only caring that they should be in the right place at the right time. Instead of the familiar clothes they wore at rehearsals, their new costumes are hampering their movements and making them self-conscious. The props and furniture are bigger or smaller or heavier than they had expected, so that suddenly they feel clumsy. Worst of all, they are expected to hang about interminably while the technical staff fuss over something which nobody else understands and which seems to make no difference anyway.

If that is what it seems like to the cast, the stage staff have even more to complain of. For the last few nights they have been losing sleep, trying to get everything ready on time. There is a problem with the electrical supply, and they are worried about blowing a fuse unless they can rearrange the lighting of Scene Two. One of the actors has become a weightwatcher, so now his robe hangs on him like a wrinkled balloon from yesterday's party, and wardrobe will have to make last-minute alterations. The little boy who comes in at the end has just lost his scroll for the umpteenth time, and the character actor has just announced that he must have a handrail because the steps are rickety. All the cast seem entirely absorbed in themselves – 'How do I look? –

'These shoes are too tight' - 'Can you hear me at the back?' - can't they ever think about the play? Here are the poor old stage staff, working their socks off, and nobody's going to be staring at them and laughing at their jokes and clapping. Nobody will come round afterwards and tell them they were better than anything in the West End. No wonder they feel resentful.

The only answer to all this is mutual respect and understanding, and the best way of achieving this is to let everybody have a go at both jobs. If Brian played a big part in the last production, it might be a good thing if he was assistant stage manager next time. Christine is a clever designer, we all know, but, if she has a go at playing a lady in waiting once in a while, it may help her to realise how the poor actors feel. There is no better way of arousing sympathy for somebody else than by trying to do their job and, besides, it will give everyone a broader vision of the whole production.

This is ideal advice, but of course it isn't always possible. It may be that you can't spare Brian or Christine from the work they do so well. They may even refuse to do anything else and you may not feel in a strong enough position to put your foot down. What you must do, however, is to prevent that apartheid from growing up between the cast and the stage staff. Unless they work together willingly and in good humour, your production will suffer. What is more, you are supposed to be a Christian company. Here is a great opportunity for brotherly love.

What are we going to wear ?

So you have chosen your play, decided on the staging, appointed your director, settled on your cast and the stage management team but. . . what about the costumes? Who is going to be in charge of them?

As we have said, you will need at least one volunteer to take on this responsibility because it is so important. You may need more than one – someone to design the costumes and several others to make them up. This, latter, will be a hard-working job and they may lose hours of sleep trying to get everything stitched together in time for the dress rehearsal.

The designer should be prepared to work hand in glove with the director at all times and the director's decision should be final. In a small group the work of both director and designer is often taken on by the same person, but the director/designer cannot ever be expected to undertake the task of making the costumes. Here is a splendid opportunity to include some of the more elderly in the congregation who will love to help and feel themselves to be a part of your production.

Although the play and its meaning will always be the paramount consideration for your group, costumes play a vital part in its presentation and immediate effect on the audience. And in churches, especially, where it is almost impossible to arrange for scenery, it is the costumes which will catch the eyes of the audience and attract attention from all the other eye-catching objects in a church . . . the organ, the polished woodwork, the stained-glass windows, the stone carving . . . and help to fix them on the play.

Besides, your actors will be concerned at the outset with that over-shadowing question 'What am I going to wear?' There is always the fun of 'dressing up' which is one of the minor attractions of taking part in a play. But there is also the fear of making a fool of oneself, and the careful designer will make allowances and not try to force very stout Mabel into a white nightdress and a wobbly halo, or timid Mr Beverley into a purple robe which trips him up and a crown which falls over his eyes when he looks down at his feet.

A lot depends on whether your play is historical or modern. Let's consider the historical play first and suppose that it has a Biblical theme set in Old Testament times.

There is a temptation to think of such plays as easy to dress. A few old curtains draped round the shoulders for the grandees; while all we need is blankets for characters like Abraham – and the effect has been made! But it isn't quite as simple as that. Nor are the illustrations to our Bibles always accurate about the clothes of those days. A conscientious designer will take pains to find out exactly the kind of clothes these Old Testament characters would have worn, at the same time paying attention to the problems and prejudices of the actors who will be wearing the designs.

One of the most accurate sources for such costumes is to be found in Victorian paintings of the period. These painters went to great lengths to establish accuracy, and any public library will be able to supply books or reproductions. Local museums and art galleries may have Victorian paintings of Biblical scenes and are worth a visit. Books on costume can help, though most of these concentrate on the past eight hundred years. They are essential if the play falls within that period. Plays such as *A Man for All Seasons* or *Murder in the Cathedral* should provide many opportunities for accurate costuming.

But for the purpose of this chapter we are thinking in terms of a Biblical play. Your main deciding factor will, of course, be 'How much can I spend on the costumes?' If your budget is very generous you will be able to buy materials and make from scratch. If, as in most cases, you will find it difficult to make ends meet, then you will think first in terms of what you can beg or borrow from others.

All members of the drama group could be invited to bring any suitable materials (yes, in some cases these *could* be curtains!), which can be unpicked and resewn into robes or headdresses. Bits of jewellery, belts, sandals, etc., are all useful. Inevitably, designs for your costumes have to be a balance between what is desirable and what is practical.

Having settled on what can and cannot be recycled from the group's curtains, tablecloths, evening dresses, shawls, dressing-gowns and the like, and having established how much money is available for buying fresh lengths of material, the designer has to consider very carefully the effect of the shapes and colours of the costumes when they are put together. It's important for the designer to be sufficiently familiar with the play to be sure about which characters will be placed next to which other characters in any given scene. Costumes react on each other much as actors do and can look good together or jar. It's often helpful to make cut-outs of the painted designs, paste these on to cardboard and stand them up together to get the effect of the actors moving about in the different scenes.

Think carefully about colour schemes. There is a temptation to run riot with colours when dealing with the Old Testament. If you want to achieve a kind of Scheherazade effect, don't overdo it. Keep any display of fireworks for one particular and significant scene and you will have the audience stretching their eyes; but give them nothing but a rainbow palette and they will grow weary of too much colour.

It is often more telling to follow some general colour-range rather than to use all the shades in the paintbox at once. Dutch painters of the seventeenth century achieved dramatic effects by using browns, umbers, rusts and golds with an occasional dash of scarlet. Early Italian painters gave their scenes a luminous quality through the use of off-white touched with blues and dark reds. The Pre-Raphaelites used summer colours, greens, blues and deep pinks for many of their pictures. Yes, *do* go to the painters, not only for accuracy, but for their use of colour. Observe the speaking of one colour to another. What does pink have to say to brown? Does yellow always shout to red? Do buffs and greys whisper together? Do blues and purples sing? Does black startle with a cry? Do all the greens speak peace?

Take some time at the weekends wandering around picture galleries or going to bookshops to look at those expensively bound coffee-table books of the great masters, or get them out of the library to take home. You may find colours coming to you in a new light. And not only colour, but texture, is important. Choose your materials with an eye to their coarseness, smoothness, silkiness, lightness or weight. The clothes do not make the play, but they *do* underline its significance if each character is defined more sharply by the costumes you have designed for them.

Think very carefully about how much your costumes assist the actors in creating character. We have talked about the need for actors not to be dependent on their costumes and how they should rehearse as if they *were* in costume; nevertheless once the costume is on, and if the actor's body has been prepared for the costume, it will enhance the performance and help the audience to understand the play. Not only the colour, but the shape and style of a costume can be of help to the actor whose physique isn't right for the part. Suppose you have diffident young Leonard, who has an excellent speaking voice but is physically not ideal for the part of the tyrant, King Herod. How can his costume make him seem taller and more imposing? The crown will give him height, his robes can be padded on the shoulders to make him seem burly, and, if his shoes have high heels, that will complete the effect. Of course, he will have been imagining himself into a different physique, but the costume will help to enhance his imagination and give him confidence.

Then there is Barbara, the leader of the Brownies, who has been cast for Delilah. She has no natural sympathy for the character, being at heart an independent young woman who despises finery. In her difficult task of identifying herself with a scheming beauty, she will be enormously helped by a costume which is silky and diaphanous, by bracelets and anklets and jewels in her hair.

It is likely that you may run into trouble with some of the cast once their costumes are shown to them, and for this reason it's wise to let them see the designs at an early stage. Otherwise they may come as something of a shock. Leonard may feel he looks a 'bit of a Charlie' in a crown, and Barbara may protest at becoming a 'female stereotype'. Other actors may have all sorts of reasons for protesting against what the designer has planned for them: 'The colour doesn't suit me'; 'It makes me look like a pudding'; 'I shan't be able to move in all this'. If you wait for the costume-fitting, tempers and nerves may be strained and people may say things which they afterwards regret. You will need both patience and firmness. Patience, to put yourself in their place and judge whether or not their complaint is justified, and, if it *is*, to modify your design; and firmness to let them know you are not prepared to give them anything else, if you really feel they are simply being difficult.

We have said nothing, so far, about plays which are non-Biblical. For instance, you might have chosen to present *St Joan* or *The Lady's not for Burning*, which would call for distinctive costumes of the period. For the former you will run into the problems of creating armour and the heavily embroidered coronation robes for the Dauphin; for the latter you will find yourself looking for costumes which are well cut and elegant. Of course you may be fortunate enough to secure the services of a really brilliant designer in which case these plays will give him or her a chance to display imaginative talent. But assuming that no such person is available your best course would be to hire costumes for the production.

It isn't the purpose of this book to recommend hiring companies. But do remember that these can be very varied in scope and cost. Some give good advice and are moderate in price, so it's a sensible plan to shop around before settling on any one company. When you finally decide on which you will use, make sure you know exactly what the terms for hiring are, and that their estimate of costs will include all extras such as shoes, stockings, hats, belts, etc. You may find that local repertory or established amateur companies are willing to hire from their wardrobes. But don't settle on the first hire service that comes your way. You will find advertisements in *Amateur Stage*, *The Alternative Theatre Year Book*, *The Stage* and other theatrical periodicals.

Often it is almost impossible for the actors to be given their costumes before the first dress rehearsal, but they will need to get some feel of what they will be wearing before that. Here the director can be of help to his cast by ensuring that they wear something akin to what they will be wearing 'on the night'. If the women are to be in long skirts, don't let them rehearse in short ones, or in slacks. If the men are robed, suggest that they rehearse in dressing-gowns; if cloaked, then let them drape their overcoats round their shoulders.

Shoes, too, should be thought about during rehearsal. The actress who has been rehearsing in high heels will find all her movements strained when she has to put on flat sandals. Actors who will be wearing boots for their parts should rehearse in boots of their own; and those whose parts demand bare feet should take off their shoes when they rehearse. Naturally these costume aids need not be used till books are out of hands and lines learnt accurately.

The same applies to hand props. Let your cast bring things which are similar to the hand props they will be using. Bags, gloves, umbrellas, swords, daggers, shields and many other vital accessories need to be rehearsed with the actors using related objects. Remember that the characters in a play are familiar with their swords, shields, sunshades or whatever. Your actors will not be so familiar and the sight of a professional Roman soldier fumbling for his dagger can produce an unwelcome comedy effect.

Costumes can often decide the walk of the character. Too often one sees a young actress in a long dress striding as if in slacks ; or an actor stepping out in a long robe as if he were wearing a city suit. So give everyone as much of a chance as possible to rehearse in similar clothes and to handle props as like as possible to those which will be worn and handled eventually.

A very great number of plays suitable for performance in churches are contemporary. 'Thank goodness we don't have to bother about costumes for the play!' is often the reaction of the director when given a modern play to produce. And the play gets put on with a group of actors wearing whatever clothes they thought would 'do', which look as mixed a bag of assorted colours and shapes as could be found on a rail in the Portobello Road on a Sunday afternoon.

Suppose you were directing *The Way of the Cross* by Henri Ghéon or *Christ in the Concrete City* by Philip Turner. In both plays you have a group of contemporary men and women following the story of the Crucifixion not only through their own experience but through the experience of other people. How would you dress them? They have to speak for characters other than their own. They don't want to look too realistic. It's tempting to say to the cast, 'Just come in trousers or skirts with a simple pullover', and they will look about as undistinguished as a queue at the bus-stop. It may be that you want to give the impression of their being just ordinary men and women picked at random from any street in the world. After all, the plays are both universal. But they will be making a picture. Think of the blending of dark reds, slate blues and sombre greys which make up the figures of an industrial landscape painted by Lowry. He is showing us just ordinary men, women and children on the streets. But he is making a picture out of them.

Use your modern clothes, then, to make a picture. Ask your cast (and their friends, if necessary), to bring an assortment of possible garments for their parts in the modern play. If possible, let them leave you alone with this assortment to enable you to experiment with them, putting this suit with that dress, this pair of jeans with that Indian skirt. Whatever happens, don't let yourself be rushed into settling on any piece of clothing which a particular actor may fancy wearing. If it is impossible for you to be left with the pile of clothing, then perhaps you could make brief sketches of them and make your experiments with the sketches when you get home.

The picture you make will, of course, need to be a subtle one. And here again the use of colour combinations can be effective. Try limiting costumes to, say, greys, dark reds and inky blues, and the result will be telling. Your audience may not even be aware of the picture you are deliberately creating, but somewhere in their unconsciousness they will respond to the discipline of your colour range and will find the picture satisfying.

Once again, visit your local picture gallery or museum and borrow or buy art books. But this time head for the twentieth-century section. Note the colours used by painters such as Stanley Spencer, David Hockney or Richard Hamilton – to take three painters whose colour-scales vary widely from each other – and make notes of the paintings which you, yourself, find most compelling. Gradually you will develop the eye that is needed for a costume designer. Don't worry too much that you haven't been allowed a generous budget. Professional designers sometimes suffer from having too much money to spend. A designer can often produce wonderful results from the ingenuity required to manage on a shoe-string. Have you thought of using black and white? Or brown and black? Or all shades of blue? Your costumes will look just like those worn by people at a bus-stop, but, because you have made a picture out of them, the audience will focus their attention more sharply on the play.

Make-up

Closely connected with the subject of costume is make-up, which hardly justifies a whole chapter in this book. In fact, the keynote of this brief section will be caution. Theatrical make-up is less and less in vogue on the professional stage, and amateurs are well advised to follow that example. In particular, it is only too easy to overdo it, and you may sometimes see actors in village halls in make-up that would be generous at the Coliseum.

This warning applies a hundredfold in church, where too much make-up looks not only strange but in poor taste. If possible, the rule should be that no one in the audience can guess you are made up at all. Indeed, if the performance is given by daylight or even by the normal artificial lighting of the church, you are probably wise to keep away from either greasepaint or pancake. A woman may slightly exaggerate her normal street make-up, if she wears one; if not, she may decide to make up lightly for the show. For men, the restraint should be even greater; the most a man should normally allow himself for ordinary lighting is a slight darkening of the eyebrows and the upper lip, a very thin dark line along the edge of the upper eyelid, and a gentle application of mascara to the upper eyelashes.

Remember that the purpose of this kind of make-up is not to make you look different or more attractive, but simply to emphasise those parts of the face with which you make signals, so that they carry the message over a greater distance. We, in the audience, need to be affected by your eyes and mouth, but that does not mean that we ought to be conscious of them. Still less should we be distracted by admiring your personal charm. The days when every actor had to be conventionally handsome, every actress outstandingly beautiful are over; the theatre of today demands expressiveness rather than beauty.

If the show is being given under theatrical lighting, brought in specially for the purpose, then perhaps you may be a little bolder and wear a thin base of colour, with a slight heightening of cheeks and lips and even a faint brush of eyeshadow, but again the intention must be that nobody should notice what you have done. When in doubt, it is much better to wear too little make-up than too much.

In any case, your make-up is not a private matter, any more than your costume. It must blend with that of the other actors, so that you all look natural together. For that reason, every single make-up should be inspected under the lighting during – or, better still, immediately before – the dress rehearsal, and then be duly altered if necessary. Ideally, other people besides the director may wish to have a voice. The designer should be there to see how the make-up blends with the costumes, and the electrician to see how it looks under the lights; both of these may be able to make valuable suggestions.

Even the simplest make-up demands skill, which takes a good deal of practice to perfect, so that it is quite possible that some of your group may not be very deft at it, in which case it is best to let someone else make them up. This not only avoids the danger of people coming on with bright orange faces or smudged and droopy eyes; it also helps to give the make-up the same kind of unity that you want for the costumes. Not surprisingly, women tend to be better than men at making up, and some groups have one woman member who makes up the entire cast, but there is something to be said for having a man to do the men and a woman to do the women. For some reason, it is much more difficult to make up the opposite sex, and in any case it is far easier and quicker to have the men and women made up separately, though of course you must make sure that your two make-up artists are working together in harmony.

The most commonly available forms of theatrical make-up are greasepaint and pancake, both of which ought to be on sale in at least one of the chemists of your nearest sizeable town. If you can't find them, ask someone in a local theatre, amateur dramatic group or school where they put on plays; they must get their supplies from somewhere. Failing them, the County Drama Adviser should be able to help you - ring the offices of your County Council to find out if they've got one - and in the last resort you will find some addresses to write to at the back of this book.

Of the two, greasepaint is slightly messier to use, and it is important to make sure that the costumes are carefully protected from it. Some people make up before dressing. Others wear a little plastic make-up cape, which you can buy at any chemist, while others drape a towel round their shoulders. But don't assume that your problems are over when your make-up is complete. The first thing to do is to wash your hands thoroughly; if (as only too often) there is no water in the church, little freshening pads, like Quickies, are perfectly adequate. And always remember that, if your hands are clean, your face is not. If you kiss somebody, you may leave traces behind you, and, if you have to cry on somebody's shoulder, you must be careful not to touch their costume, or you will stain it.

If you are using greasepaint, the first thing to do is rub a thin layer of grease or cream onto your face. The best known preparation is Cremine, but almost any foundation cream will do, and, if you are not too particular, you can even make do with lard. The important word, however, is thin. When you have rubbed it well in, wipe off the remainder with a tissue, so that your face hardly feels greasy at all.

The base colour is applied with sticks, usually in combinations of two or more. Number 5 (ivory) is the basic medium, into which to mix Number 8 or Number 9 for men, Number 2½ or Number 3 for women. There are, of course, a great variety of colours to choose from, and with experience you may want to vary this rather dull formula, but there are great advantages about using a combination of two sticks. It enables you to vary the colour subtly over the face, so that you don't look as if you have been given a coat of plastic emulsion paint.

Once you have achieved the right base, you should concentrate on the modelling of the face, picking out the highlights very faintly with Number 5 or Number 1½ and very slightly darkening the parts you want to seem in shadow. For this you can use the darker of the two colours of your base, possibly deepened by the merest touch from a liner of Brown, Blue or Lake (dark red). This process is very easily overdone, so use only the lightest touch.

The liners are thinner, pointed sticks of greasepaint, intended for putting in details rather than painting broad effects, but even then they will not be fine enough for all your purposes, and you will need a few orange-sticks to thrust into the colour you want and transfer it delicately to the face. Orange-sticks are particularly useful for the fine detail round the mouth and eyes, but the lines of paint should never be left hard-edged but smoothed softly so as to be undetectable at a distance.

For women, two shades of lipstick are better than one; the mouth looks much more natural if the upper lip is darker than the lower. For a man, try not to think in terms of lipstick as such. Instead, put the darker base colour pure on the upper lip, and for the lower add the merest hint of red or pink to the surrounding base.

This is the stage for women to put on eye-shadow. With green, blue and lake liners, it is possible to mix most of the colours currently worn, or you can use ordinary eye-shadow, if you buy the type in greasy sticks like lipstick. Once again, unless you are playing Jezebel, you should avoid using too much or too startling a colour. For men this caution is even more important, and the most a man should allow himself is a little Number 8 or brown liner, smeared along the upper eyelid with the tip of a finger.

Now take an ordinary eyebrow pencil, bought at the chemist, black if you are dark or brown if you are fair. Very gently emphasise the shape of the eyebrow, and then draw a fine line along the very edge of the upper eyelid, immediately above the lashes. Both sexes should do this, but only women who wish to look made up should put one along the edge of the lower lid as well. Now put mascara on the lashes of your upper lid, and here you can be reasonably generous. You may even try putting a little on your lower lashes as well, but this is very difficult, and, if your eyes water during the show, you may get black streaks running down your cheeks.

Finally the whole effect should be powdered over with blending powder, but this too can be overdone. Too much powder will make your face look as if it is made of velour. Brush away any surplus with a very soft brush, applied with a light hand, so as not to disturb the painting underneath. And Now – in the words of a well-known notice – Wash Your Hands.

By contrast, theatrical pancake, which is water-based, is rather easier to apply. It is sold in little round flat tins in a great variety of shades, some of which are quite difficult to tell apart, and also in sticks. A generally sound base colour for women is Kryolan 3W and for men Kryolan 5W. Begin by washing and drying your face, then pour a little water into the lid of the tin, moisten a little make-up sponge, rub it over the pancake, and then apply it to your face. Provided you don't spill the water or drop the sponge (both surprisingly easy to do) this is a much cleaner method of making up. With the pansticks it is even easier.

Unfortunately, water-based make-up has disadvantages. When it dries, your face can look a little like a painted wall. If it does, you can polish it with a chamois leather, soft cloth, or even with the ball of your thumb, until your skin has a pleasing sheen. Then, of course, you still have the detail to do, for which you can use greasepaint, though now you have lost the advantages of cleanliness. In film and television studios, the make-up artists use pancake very sparingly, so that parts of your natural skin show through, and then often go on to paint delicately on top of the base from a paintbox of shadowy colours, laid on with a sable brush.

Since the recent change in women's make-up styles, this kind of paintbox is now quite widely on sale, and you may enjoy experimenting with one. You can also buy compressed rouges and eye-shadows in a surprising range of colours, and these will also lie quite happily on top of theatrical pancake. Once again, the important point is subtlety, which is best achieved by only the most delicate contrasts, divided by soft edges. With pancake, you do not need to use much, if any, powder.

Nowadays there is a very popular type of make-up called aquacolour, which is easy and flexible, but it has one very serious disadvantage for use in churches – it is comparatively obvious. If you are playing in a cathedral under a full lighting board, it will be fine, but you will find it difficult not to give yourself away in a small church, especially if you have to pass very close to the audience.

Up till now, we have been talking about 'straight' make-up, in which you are only trying to make your appearance slightly more vivid. Most of the books hurry through this section in their excitement to get to the really interesting parts, such as how to disguise a young man as an octogenarian and the art of looking Chinese. This is a fascinating study, and Roy Dotrice gave us a brilliant example for his performance in *Brief Lives*, but you may not find it very useful in your church group.

For one thing, it is easier to act convincingly if you are playing your own physical type, and, for another, voice and movement are far more important tools than make-up in suggesting any change. Besides, in church your audience will almost certainly know you, so that at first sight they will think not 'This is Esau,' but 'Here comes old Neville in a red beard.' If you are going to persuade them that you really are Esau, you will do it by getting them to join in your own imaginative leap, and for that purpose the beard may actually get in the way.

That is not the end of the troubles. Very heavy make-ups can produce practical problems of their own. Shadows and highlights which look natural in repose may seem curiously distorted when your face becomes mobile. A violent grimace can actually bring loose a false beard; to our horror, we actually saw this happen recently at a preview on the London stage. Other things being equal, it is usually better to settle for your cast looking roughly the way they do in normal life.

Even so, there will be times when you have to disguise somebody. The play has a scene for Simeon, and your oldest member is thirty, the woman who is going to wash Jesus' feet wears her hair short, or the Virgin comes on first as a young girl and finally as an old lady.

The possibilities are so endless that it would need a whole book to cover them properly, and you had better buy a book on the subject or borrow one from the library. We have suggested some titles at the end of this book. In the meantime, here are a few general observations.

Wigs are now sold widely and are tolerably cheap to buy, though you will be lucky to get anything worth looking at for much under twenty pounds. Moreover, they are intended to look attractive, which may not be what you want. There are a number of firms who hire theatrical wigs, but their standards vary considerably, and the best are not at all cheap.

Beards and moustaches cannot be hired; they must be bought, and again the standards vary, usually with the price. You can, however, make them for yourself out of crepe hair. This can be bought wherever you buy make-up and is not really difficult to use, provided you are neat-fingered and follow certain definite rules. Before use, crepe hair must be straightened in a jet of steam from the kettle, and it is generally best to mix two or more colours, rather than using black, brown, red or white on its own.

Cut the hair roughly to length and stick it to the skin with spirit gum (which stings some skins) or rubber solution (which smells dreadful). Put it on a bit at a time, laying it neither at right angles to the skin nor flat along it but at a natural angle. Remember that a beard normally grows not only from the jaw but also from the throat. Keep it dense, unless you want a sparse effect, and trim it to the exact shape when the gum has set.

Putting on false hair should be done after making up, but it will stick better if the area beneath it is free from make-up. Remember that there is nothing to hold it together, so the tip of every hair must be imbedded in the gum. Taking a beard of crepe hair off again can be a painful process, but, if you do it carefully, you may be able to use the beard again another day. Put on with rubber solution, it may even last for years.

In tackling the rest of a character make-up, once again be guided by caution. Even the best books tend to be run away with by their enthusiasm to give the old lady eyes like craters or the middle-aged merchant a blue chin. You would be wiser to stick to the principle that the audience should not notice the make-up. After the first few minutes, they are not going to think about it anyway, and it is your job to suggest rather than to proclaim the character that the actor is going to portray.

Staging and setting

The Catholic and Anglican liturgy, the Free Church sermon, are all forms of drama in their way, and many churches are deliberately dramatic buildings. A performance can gain great impact by being played in church; the towering architecture, the shadowy distances, the mysterious atmosphere of transcendence combine impressively to work on the feelings of the audience.

England has perhaps the largest collection of beautiful churches in the world. They make a wonderful setting and offer all kinds of dramatic opportunities. The pulpit, the rood screen, the sanctuary, the organ loft, may be turned into unexpected standpoints for the actors, voices can come from behind the audience, processions can move up the aisles, great doors can open and slam.

Nevertheless, hardly any churches have been designed for the kind of stage performance we think of today. In almost every one, there are practical problems to be solved, if the audience are not to be like the heathen idols of the Psalmist: 'Eyes have they, but they see not: They have ears, but they hear not.'

The first essential of any church production is to make sure that the audience can see what you want them to see and hear what you want them to hear. Neither of these need be a grave difficulty if the audience is small and sitting close to the action, but they will never be easy, and, as your popularity grows and your numbers increase, they will become harder.

Seeing and hearing are closely related, but it will be easier to consider them separately, so this chapter is concerned with the question: *What can the audience see?*

The first question is, of course, how much you want them to see, and, though the answer may be 'as much as possible', that is not always the case. Nearly every production has something to be concealed: the performers waiting to make their entrances, the prompter and the technicians, hidden in dark corners. Some plays will depend much more on sound than sight, and there may even be productions where you do not want any details to be seen at all, as for example the blend of lighting, music and voices in *son et lumière*.

On the other hand, the very fact that the spoken voice is not always perfectly clear in church makes the visual element even more important than in the secular theatre. The sight of the performers, the movement and the glow of light will help to concentrate the attention of the audience, and they will actually hear better for seeing clearly. Striking costumes may help to light their imaginations, and the sight of physical action is often more emotive than words.

Once you have chosen what you want to be seen, you must decide where it will be most visible. In many churches, there will be a number of obstructions. Norman pillars can effectively cut off all vision from the north and south aisles, and even the slenderest Perpendicular will spoil the view from some seats. A narrow arch may obscure half the chancel from one side of the nave, and of course the pulpit and lectern are effective hazards. You will be lucky if you find you can move either of them.

In many buildings, you will find very little choice of position. If there are fixed pews, you will obviously have to play in front of them, and the space for your acting area may be narrowly confined by screens and stalls. In churches with movable chairs, there are many more options. You may decide to turn the audience round and perform at the back or, in a large cruciform priory, you may prefer the more intimate space of one of the transepts. Wherever you finally hold the performance, you will have to consider the view from every seat. If it is difficult or impossible to see from some of them, you would be well advised to block them off or put warning notices on them.

The next problem is height. The average person, sitting in a pew, is about three feet six inches high, with an eye level about six inches lower at three feet. This means that the person sitting in front of you seems about six inches higher than you are, so in the normal way you adjust your position to look over their shoulder.

As the church fills up, this grows more difficult, especially if you are not near the front. The average head is about seven inches broad, while the average body takes up about twenty-one inches of pew. This means that, when the audience gets really packed, you can only enjoy an uninterrupted view by sitting in the front row. Move back one row, and you lose a third of your vision. From the next it will be two thirds. From the fourth row backwards you will be peering over an unbroken wall of heads, a barrier six inches high and at best three rows in front.

A few churches have raked seating for the congregation, and rather more have a well-raised chancel, but these are the exceptions. Most mediaeval or Victorian churches are either completely flat or rise by only one or two steps. This means that, if you are expecting to fill more than the front three pews, you must make sure the performers are raised above their audience if you want them to be seen.

How high? A quick answer to this question is often to look at the floor of the pulpit. In Victorian churches especially, the preacher was intended to be seen, and was raised up accordingly. Unfortunately, this is not an infallible rule. Some early pulpits are absurdly high, and many modern ones rather too low. It is safer to calculate by the following formula.

Begin by counting the number of rows you expect to be occupied. If there is a row missing to make a passage across the church, or if there is room for one or more rows between the stage and the front pew, then you must count those too, just as if they were really there. Now, multiply the number by two inches and add three feet. Thus for six rows the answer will be four feet, for eleven it will be five feet, and so on.

This measurement is the height below which virtually nothing will be visible to the man sitting in the back row, and you may find the answer surprisingly high. For instance, in a church of twenty-four rows he is unlikely to see anything below seven feet. It would be nice for him if you built the stage as high as that, but it would not be very pleasant for the people in front; they would have to strain their heads back to see anything at all, and the front of the stage would cut off much of their view. In fairness to all parties, you will have to settle for a compromise.

For practical purposes, the utmost height for a church stage is about four feet six inches, and three feet is a great deal better for the front rows. It is also safer for the performers, easier to borrow, or cheaper to build. Local schools often possess sectional staging, three feet high, and can sometimes be prevailed upon to lend it, provided you can arrange transport.

A height of only three feet in a flat church is going to put physical limitations on your production. If a performer kneels on the floor or sits on a chair, his face will be fully visible only to the first eighteen rows of a packed church, only to the first twelve if he sits on the floor. Moreover, the audience wants to see more than the performers' faces; gestures and movement will only be really visible when the actor stands up.

For this reason, there is a good deal to be said for a stage on different levels, rising from, say, three feet at the front to six or seven feet upstage. This will give people at the back of the church the chance to see important characters from head to foot, without putting undue strain on the front rows. However there are disadvantages about multi-level stages; they tend to dictate your style and even your choice of play. Formalised work can be very effective on them, but they give a curiously disturbing quality to naturalistic drama. Beware, too, of the danger of falling off the back!

Whatever kind of stage you choose, make sure that it is level, steady, safe and silent. Church floors are often uneven, and there is nothing more disconcerting than acting on a collection of blocks that rock noisily and independently whenever you make a move. A very good form of wedge is paper, often in the form of old church magazines; there is very little spring in it, and because it is divided into pages, you can control the thickness to a hundredth of an inch. With any form of wedging, however, it is slow, patient work to make a sectional stage really steady on an uneven floor.

You will also need broad safe steps for getting on and off the stage. Try them out well in advance; going up is easy, but coming down is a very different matter, especially with stage lights to dazzle you.

Now that you have got your stage, what are you going to put on it? Most stage performances have scenery or at the very least a surround of curtains, but anything of that sort would be throwing away one of your biggest single assets, the special quality of the building. A church production has no use for a box set or a backcloth and wings, far less for a proscenium or front curtain. Quite apart from the fact that very few clergy would allow such a thing, any form of full setting would obscure the character of the church itself, by hiding the windows, pillars and furniture with something that can hardly help being less attractive. It is almost impossible for constructions in timber and painted canvas to avoid looking tawdry when surrounded by mediaeval stone, Victorian glass or Georgian panelling. In the cool, spare concrete churches of today, it is even more difficult to get away with that kind of theatrical scenery.

There is, however, a valuable place for what is called detail setting. This means the use of one or two objects to suggest the scene you are trying to portray without setting it out in full. Such suggestive details can fire the imagination of the audience. We have already considered two examples of this kind in our play about the Prodigal: the table and chairs for Scene One and the Chinese lantern in Scene Two. In fact, the range is almost infinite, and there are very few scenes that cannot be suggested by one or two details.

Take, for example, the kind of stage directions you are all too apt to find at the beginning of a religious play:

> *Night.* THREE SHEPHERDS *are sitting on a bleak hillside, sparsely covered with turf. Their tent of skins trembles in the cold breeze, and the men are huddling round a smoulder-*

*ing brazier at its mouth. Behind them rises a jagged outcrop
of rock. As the moon comes out from behind a cloud, a
man can be seen laboriously struggling to climb the summit,
where he stands and shouts against the wind to his com-
panions.*

DISTANT SHEPHERD: What of the night?

The picture is vivid enough, but it reads like a film. Even in the
theatre it would be difficult to produce an effect quite like that; you
cannot hope to do it in a church. Quite apart from the question of
expense, the background would make it look absurd, and, besides,
how are we going to clear it away? We've got the stable coming, and
Herod's palace later.

For the moment, ignore the stage directions and simply read the
scene. What is the basic minimum that we need? The opening dialogue
is all about the cold wind on the barren hillside. No great problem here;
like Shakespeare, the author has described the general setting, so we
don't need to show it as well. Then there is a fear that a lamb has been
lost, and the Old Shepherd asks the Shepherd Boy to fetch him his
crook –

OLD SHEPHERD: Bring me my crook, lad. You will find it in the tent.

So we do need the tent after all, but there seems to be no reason why
it should not be offstage. The Boy can simply disappear and come back
with the crook, and the existence of the tent has been established. The
jagged outcrop is another matter; at a later stage, the Angel is going to
appear on it with wonderful news. The author seems to expect him to
descend from Heaven, which is more than we can manage, but it would
be nice if he were on a higher level than the other characters. At the
same time, we don't want to be stuck with a jagged rock all through the
Bethlehem and Herod scenes.

A rostrum, three feet high and four feet square, can probably be
borrowed from a nearby school and will make a good compromise,
especially if we can have a set of steps in front of it and a smaller,
eighteen-inch rostrum behind, so that the actors can get up the back
without looking clumsy. It will do for our jagged rock now, and perhaps we could put Herod's throne on it later. Of course it won't look
at all realistic, but then nothing could, set in the middle of a church.
You will have to convince the audience of the existence of the hillside by other means, most of all by the acting. If the actor looks as if
he is rock-climbing, and if all four are quite clear about which way the
wind is blowing, that will have far more effect than any amount of
canvas rock or plastic grass.

The one thing we do really want is the brazier. There are continual references to it in the script, and it clearly has to be in the centre of the action. Look at this: –

DISTANT SHEPHERD (*drawing closer*): Let me sit by the fire, young fellow. My bones are frozen by this bitter air. (*squatting over the brazier*) I looked up from the valley and saw the glow on the hillside. It will surely keep the wolves many miles away.

OLD SHEPHERD: Then don't cover it all with your cloak. It serves for a light as well as for warmth.

After all that, and much more besides, it would be a great pity not to have a visible fire. The Shepherds have cloaks, so perhaps they could bring on a metal waste-paper-basket with holes drilled in the sides, painted black and lined with orange filters and with a light inside it.

Described like that, it sounds appallingly tatty, but in fact it will have to be very carefully made. For one thing, we don't want to trail a flex across the stage, so the light will have to be run from a battery inside, but the switch will have to be on the outside, so that it can be switched on when the brazier is in position. The filters will have to be fixed quite firmly, so that there is no leak of white light round the orange glow. The whole thing will have to be heavy enough for people to huddle round it with no risk of knocking it over, but light enough to be carried unobtrusively under a cloak. With any luck we can manage with very little other light indeed, but the outside must be convincing enough to bear inspection by the front rows.

Here we come to one of the most important advantages of detail setting. The fact that each detail is small in size means that it can be either the genuine article or at least made to a far higher standard than you could lavish on a full-scale set. It does not matter so much that it should be realistic – in fact, it is often an advantage for it to be completely formalised – as that it should be attractive in itself. In the church you may be surrounded by examples of the highest craftsmanship. Against such a background, any botched additions of your own will be cruelly exposed.

It may be that for some scenes you will want to go beyond what could be strictly described as a detail. Perhaps you feel that for the next scene of this Nativity you really must build a stable. The manger is a vital part of the script, and you want to suggest the cattle lurking in the shadows. The text is quite clear that the stable is light, while the Shepherds hesitate outside in the darkness, and how are you to achieve all this unless you have some kind of building?

Very good, but first you must consider the difficulties. How are you going to bring it on, and how will you get it off again? There is no curtain for the stagehands to hide behind, and screens are an awkward alternative which look out of place in most churches. Blackout is next to impossible and almost always undesirable. You are left with two possibilities. Either you bring it on (or build it) before the eyes of your audience, or you keep it onstage for the whole play.

Whichever you choose, and both have disadvantages, you will make your life much easier (not to mention the lives of your designer, carpenter and stage manager, if you are lucky enough to have them all) if you remember that your building must be formalised. For one thing, there is the question of height. In real life, most stables are at least fifteen feet high, whereas you would be very ambitious to make it more than seven. Read the text carefully. How many people have to be in there at once? Are they standing or kneeling? This little inner stage will gain in power by being like a tiny jewel of light in the surrounding darkness.

Then again, what is it to be made of? It is not easy to make a convincing imitation of a stone building, when you are surrounded by the real thing, but, so long as you make no attempt at naturalism, this problem need not worry you. The audience will be invited to use their imagination, and there is no point in jogging their elbow.

Perhaps you feel it is very important that there should be no light leaks, in which case the back, sides and top of the stable will have to be built solid. That puts an end to any question of bringing it or building it onstage. It will have to be there from the beginning, and it might even do double duty for the Shepherds' tent. With a framework constructed out of 2 x 1 timber (this is minimal; the professional theatre always use 3 x 1) and covered with cloth or cardboard, sealed with gaffer tape and carefully painted, your stable should be reasonably rigid and lightproof, but it will not stand moving about.

Alternatively you might borrow from the Oriental tradition of theatre and offer us nothing but a roof supported by an outline. This would be light enough to carry onstage if you want to, but you might prefer to have a curtain along the front of the eaves. Then you could still use it for the Shepherds' tent, with the curtain drawn, and open it to reveal the stable in Scene Two. The light can be concealed in the crook of the roof, shining down onto the interior and throwing up a soft glow of reflections all around. Or you might even hide a light in the manger itself, shining upwards into the face of Mary.

Herod's throne presents the other great problem: how can you do anything grand enough? Covering an old chair with gold paint leads to very disappointing results. If it was going to be there from the beginning, we could simply cover a crate with a velvet drape, but this will have to be brought onstage, not surreptitiously like the brazier, but ostentatiously by two soldiers. It may be that the church itself has a handsome, timeless chair, which will serve your purpose admirably. Otherwise, you will have to search. Go round the houses of your friends, poke about in furniture and antique shops. Don't make too precise a picture of what you are looking for, or you may walk past the ideal thing. When you have found it, then you have the task of persuading them to lend it to you. And remember, anything you borrow should be treated with the utmost care and respect. Otherwise, nobody will want to lend to you again.

The problem of getting on and offstage does not only apply to the scenery. The actors may have to go on a very long journey within sight of the audience whenever they make an entrance or exit. Your play may demand that people dash on and off, which may in some churches involve a twenty-five yard sprint from the vestry. Attention will inevitably be drawn away from the stage by the sight of other actors coming and going.

There is no universal solution to this problem and if conditions are really against you, you will just have to make the best of a bad job. One method is to have on either side of the stage some kind of free-standing screens behind which the actors can lie in wait for their cues. The first entrance of each performer, however, will still have to be a long trek, unless you hide everybody there before the audience arrives, and it is seldom easy to find or make screens that will look at home in the church. In some buildings there will be pillars you can use in this way or even bulky choir stalls, and on winter evenings the careful use of lighting may plunge the surroundings into comparative darkness. Take care, though, that your cast do not bump into things in the dark.

Alternatively, you can seat all your performers near the stage, where they can simply get up and make their entrances when they are wanted and to which they can return after their exits. In some ways the best seats for this purpose are the front pews, the ones with no reading-desk in front of them, where it is often difficult to persuade the audience to sit anyway. Now the distance is nice and short, but there are other disadvantages. The audience are sitting one row further away from the stage than they might, and the heads of the cast will be another obstacle in the way of the sightlines. Any change of costume is of course im-possible, and the actors will have to maintain a very tight discipline whenever they are sitting out a scene. There is something very intriguing about the sight of the cast as they sit there, and those near them may find it difficult to concentrate on the action. To prevent this, the waiting performers must never allow their own attention to wander from the stage. Then the eyes of the audience will follow theirs back into the play.

Finally it is possible to make a virtue of necessity by letting the action start some way from the stage at the first point where the actors become visible. The difficulty here is that this point will vary slightly for every single member of the audience, and the people on one side of the church may be able to see an actor some yards before he comes into view from the other side. The new action will have to grow gradually, so that it is sufficiently intriguing from the first moment that anyone can see it, without becoming so important that the others will feel that they have missed something.

All the problems described in this chapter should be in your mind before you make your final choice of a play. The mere fact that you are performing in a church will affect your whole style of production, and the characteristics of your particular building may rule out some plays altogether. These difficulties apply not only to the cast but to your stage staff too. If scenery or furniture has to be moved, they will have nothing to hide behind. The stagehands will have to come onstage, frankly and unselfconsciously, to change the setting in whatever way is necessary. You may decide to dress them in the style of the actors, and sometimes you will be able to use the actors themselves. We have already suggested that soldiers should bring on Herod's throne. In a Passion Play the Elders could bring on their seats for the Sanhedrin, and soldiers could even bring on two pillars for the scene with Pilate. Even larger pieces of scenery might be brought and cleared by the crowd.

In planning your setting, you should always pause to consider whether each piece can stay in position throughout, and, if not, how they can be convincingly taken on and off. If you can find no satisfactory answer to either of these questions, then perhaps the pieces themselves are not necessary. If they are absolutely essential, but you do not know what to do with them, then it is worth asking yourself whether this is the right play for you.

Take heart, however. Very few really good plays depend entirely on physical effects, and audiences have much more imagination that we are inclined to credit them with. Don't ask too much from them in the first few minutes, and then they will gradually suspend their disbelief and accept almost any reasonable convention that you may offer. 'Think when we speak of horses that you see them, printing their proud hoofs i' the receiving earth.' So pleads the Chorus in *Henry V*, and the wonderful thing is that everybody responds to it. You have an advantage over Shakespeare. Your theatre is no cockpit or wooden O. It is the shrine where your audience come every week to draw closer to God.

Let there be light

'Lighting? Oh, surely we can't afford anything like that.' Well, every show has to be lit somehow, unless it's going to be given in complete darkness. That is not just intended as a clever catch answer; the fact is that, even if you are holding your performance in daylight, you should give some thought to the question of how light falls on the stage and its surroundings.

During the day, the light in a church is greatly affected by the shape and structure of the building. All good architects give consideration to the natural play of light, and this was a special concern of the Gothic tradition, where churches were designed not so much to fill a space as to enclose it, so that the interest is chiefly focused on the inside. In a typical parish church of the high Middle Ages, the brightest area of light was round the altar, where the drama of the Mass was to be played out. The east window might be heavily coloured, so that it had only the effect of a brightened picture, but there would be large, clearer windows on either side to throw the celebrant into sharp relief. Coming westward, the chancel would tend to grow steadily darker, brightening again a little at the chancel arch but remaining fairly low-key all the way down the nave. By comparison with a Georgian drawing-room, a mediaeval church was very dark indeed with occasional luminous splashes. Milton's 'dim religious light' was like an archetype for modern theatrical lighting.

In another quite different tradition, the Victorian dissenting chapel may actually have been copied, albeit unconsciously, from Georgian theatres. The horseshoe gallery, the narrow pillars and the elaborate woodwork at the centre of interest are reminiscent of the Richmond Theatre in Yorkshire or the old Theatre Royal, Bristol. Here the focus is not so much on the table as on the pulpit. The congregation have come not to witness a rite but to hear the Word. Nevertheless, the architect has taken a great deal of trouble to make sure that they should also be able to see the preacher. Moreover, they are expected to read their Bibles and hymn books, so the windows down the body of the church are usually tall and clear. By daylight, the worshippers are very well lit indeed.

These two extremes are of course best suited to very different styles of performance. The pageant and grandeur that suits the mystic grandeur of the Gothic may feel somehow diminished in the unsparing brilliance of a Victorian chapel, where it is much easier to present brisk intellectual comedy, much of which would be lost in the mediaeval shadows. In choosing a play to suit your particular place of worship, you must keep the question of lighting constantly in mind.

Another question about daylight performances is the time of day. Between, say 10 am and 3 pm, especially in summer, the sun will be too high to strike directly onto the acting area in most churches, and the light will be reflected on your actors, very often chiefly from the floor. This gives an attractive general illumination, not unflattering either, because the floor will act like a subtle form of footlights, to smooth out wrinkles and make the eyes glow.

On bright days, when the sun is lower in the sky, the situation can be very different, especially if your church has stained-glass windows. Then glowing lozenges of colour can creep slowly across your acting area, suddenly staining an actor crimson or leaving another to deliver his speech from the shadows. At eight o'clock on a sunny June evening, your audience may be distracted by the patterns of the west window gradually rising up from the stage to disappear at last in a sunset blaze on the vaulting. Nevertheless, such an evening can bestow its own magic on a play, especially as the sunlight begins to fade and we become aware of the theatrical lighting for the first time.

If yours is an evening performance, then, even if it starts in daylight, it is likely to end in the dark, so you will have to do something to help the audience see the play. Your first and most obvious resource is the existing lighting in the church. This may be anything these days from candles to real theatrical spotlights, so it is worth taking some time to study what the church has to offer. Even if you are planning to bring in an elaboroate system of your own, you can probably find something of value in the existing equipment, and in any case you will need to consider the 'houselights'.

Candlelight can be enchanting, especially if you are allowed to arrange the candles where you want them, but you may have difficulties with fire precautions. If the audience are not paying to come in, and provided you don't do it too often, the fire officer has no power to prevent you from lighting the play with naked flames, but the church insurance company may take a different view, and so may the clergy. Besides, candles are at best inconvenient and at worst downright dangerous. They are easily knocked over, especially by long robes, and their bright and living flames are a formidable counter-attraction to your performance.

Most churches, however, are lit by electricity, and this again will vary. In a few old-fashioned buildings naked lamp-bulbs trail at the end of yards of flex. Elsewhere you will find electric candelabra or wall-mounted brackets. Quite often nowadays the lights are set in the roof, surrounded by shiny metal reflectors to beam them in the required direction. Only the very unfortunate will hit on a church lit by fluorescent tubes, and gas lighting has now become a curiosity.

Before the first rehearsal it is well worthwhile for four people to spend at least an hour in the church after dark. The director should sit where the audience will be, while an actor and actress move about the acting area together, and the stage manager or electrician patiently tries every possible permutation of the lights. You need two people on the stage in order to see if they throw shadows on each other and, if so, how badly. You will also need to take notes. The stage manager should record where all the switches are and which lights they control. This can involve a long search and send you to the caretaker, begging for help. The director will need to make a note of the effect of all the most pleasing lighting arrangements and how each of them was achieved. With a well-briefed finger on every switch in the church, it may be possible to produce quite effective lighting changes without bringing in a single lantern from outside.

In most churches, however, your scope will be very limited unless you can add some lighting of your own. Before doing so, you will have to check whether the church power supply can stand it. This is a technical question, and the opinion of the vicar or verger is of doubtful value unless they can remember when the church was last wired or when additional electrical equipment was previously brought in. Since the Second World War, electric points have gradually been standardised, and the sight of square-pin sockets is reassuring, but do not assume that each one represents an individual 13-amp fuse. You are more likely to have struck a 30-amp ring main, which feeds every socket in the place, and it is just possible that the church is wired 3-phase, in which case you must on no account allow any kind of direct connection between two sockets.

For all these reasons there is a lot to be said for limiting your additional lighting to what can be taken off one 13-amp socket. That will give you more than you might suppose. Most English installations are 240 volts, which means that you can get a theoretical maximum of 3,120 watts out of a single socket. Six 500-watt lanterns, carefully arranged, are quite enough to light a simple production and will leave you with a reasonable margin on your one socket, though it will be important to experiment at some length beforehand to make sure that the fuse doesn't blow. Find out where the fuse-box is, try pulling out every fuse in turn to find which controls what outlets, and keep some fuse-wire handy. If the church is very modern and uses cutouts, you won't need fuse-wire, but don't feel overconfident; cutouts are very jumpy. If you are in doubt, perhaps the person who does the church wiring will take pity on you.

Granted that you have found an adequate power supply, you now have to decide what lights you want to bring in. With any luck you may be able to borrow them from a local school, an amateur dramatic society or the County Drama Adviser. If you are borrowing, you will be limited in your choice, but it is a good thing to have some understanding of what you are offered. In general, remember that modern lanterns may give twice as much illumination as their old-fashioned counterparts; also that two low-power lanterns will give you more flexibility for your wattage than one big one, but the big one will offer the longer throw.

Failing a free loan, you have the choice of hiring or buying equipment. Theatrical lighting is very expensive, and you would be most unwise to begin building up your own collection until you are quite sure that your group is going not only to survive but to present regular and frequent productions. To start off, you will do much better by hiring. Then, if things go well, you might consider buying one piece of equipment for each production, so that you need to hire progressively less and less.

However you acquire it, the lighting you are offered is likely to fall into three main categories, battens, floods and spots. In essence, a BATTEN is a long line of low-power bulbs (up to 150 watts each, but usually less) originally screwed to a length of timber (hence the name) but now more commonly enclosed in a metal trough, which may or may not be divided into compartments. In the theatre battens were at one time hung out of sight above the scenery in the area known as the 'flies', or sunk into the front of the stage as footlights, which are still sometimes called 'floats' from the days when they were burning wicks floating in a long ditch of oil.

Battens are probably the least useful form of lighting for a production in church. For one thing, they are very heavy to move about and virtually impossible to hang. Almost the only practicable use for them is as floats, which are not a suitable medium for lighting most churches, because they cast light upwards. The result looks 'theatrical' in the worst sense of the word, and the chancel roof will be only too well lit. Regard battens as a last-ditch expedient for lighting your show; almost any alternative will work better.

FLOODLIGHTS are a great deal handier to move about and are not too heavy to carry. You would be ill-advised to have anything bigger than 500 watts, which is quite easy to manage. They can be hung from a beam, strapped to a pillar, raised on a stand or even laid on the floor, so that your light can come from almost any direction you want. They give a broad wash of light over a wide angle (120° or more), and there is very little you can do to make it narrower. By pointing them slightly downwards, you can keep the light off the roof, but in that case you must have them well in front of the audience if you are to avoid lighting the front rows, and you will have to accept a wide spill of light to either side.

SPOTLIGHTS are a completely different matter. They give a relatively narrow beam (the angle can usually be adjusted between about 10° and 60°) with a great intensity of light, rather like a modified lighthouse. Like floods, they are extremely portable and can be fixed almost anywhere with ingenuity, but unlike floods they present no problems of spill. They can light exactly the area you want from the direction you choose, leaving everything else in darkness, more or less. You can place them in front, to the side or even behind the actors but still arrange them so that they do not shine into the audience. Spots are the aristocrats of the lighting world; they can do the job of almost any other form of lighting and often do it better.

Spots come in two types: profiles and Fresnels. The PROFILE spot throws a relatively hard-edged beam, not allowing a single ray to stray outside the circle of light. Its effect can be very dramatic, especially if used from the side or behind the actors, and it is particularly useful for throwing a long-distance beam from behind the audience without lighting up the backs of the front rows.

The FRESNEL spot has a corrugated lens, which softens away the sharp edges and casts a diminishing glow round the central beam. Not so good when placed out front, a Fresnel is much easier than a profile for use close to the stage, because the actors need not move through harsh and sudden changes of illumination.

It goes without saying that for all your lights you will need cables and connecting plugs and sockets. The cables should be of the thick, 'cab-tyre' variety, preferably in black, and should be placed as safely and inconspicuously as possible. Ideally, the plugs and sockets should be 15-amp round-pin, which have no fuse, though of course you will need at least one 13-amp square-pin where you plug into the wall. A system using nothing but 13-amp plugs would in theory be far safer, but it can get you into awful trouble if a fuse blows. You may spend half an hour trying to locate it, only to find that it is ten feet up a pillar.

With the use of adaptors, you can lead all the lights back to one wall socket, but 15-amp adaptors are a valuable rarity these days, and in any case it is far better if your electrician can have a PLUGBOARD, with which one can switch each light on or off without moving from one place. 13-amp plugboards can be bought quite cheaply from most hardware or electrical shops, and a 15-amp one can be made by anyone with a basic knowledge of electricity and a knack for DIY. If you are hiring your lights, then all these accessories should be supplied with them.

Far better than a plugboard, but also in a different order of price, is a DIMMER BOARD, which will enable you to raise and fade each circuit smoothly and independently from darkness to light and back again as fast or slowly as you wish. In your group you may possibly have a very good electrician who can make one for you, but it is much more likely that you will have to hire or borrow one. The old-fashioned type have SLIDERS, running up and down rheostat coils. They are sturdy and reliable, but the coils are apt to overheat if you are not careful, and in old age the sliders grow rusty and begin to squeak and jerk. The newer models work with THYRISTORS and are a good deal easier to handle, but they need much more maintenance and have a greater tendency to go wrong. Sensibly used, and provided they are in good condition, either type of dimmer board can give a wonderful flexibility to your lighting effects.

First, of course, you must put your lights in the places where you need them, and in church this can raise all kinds of problems. The easiest solution is to mount them on purpose-built STANDS, standing on the floor or, if that is not high enough, on pews or even trestle tables. There is a range of lightweight stands intended for small companies, some of them rising to twelve feet or more. Naturally you will have to take precautions that nobody knocks or pulls them over. The greatest danger is of somebody tripping over the cable, so hide it, if you can, under a carpet or grating. In old churches you will sometimes find baize runners on the pews, which make excellent cable covers. Even more important, tie the cable off at the foot of the stand and again on something immovable. Then, if anyone trips over your cable, they may shift your light but are unlikely to bring it down on their heads.

Stands are the quickest method of putting up lights, but they are not necessarily the best. In a church with traditional stone arches it is often possible to set up a first-class lighting loom on TWO-INCH BARREL, which is the technical name for the tubular steel used in scaffolding. Run the barrel between two pillars and secure it with clothes-line above the capitals. The lanterns can then be hung from the barrel on G-clamps, but be sure to use safety chains (normally supplied with all spotlights) especially if the lights are above the heads of the audience.

There are plenty of other ways of supporting lights. You can lash an angle iron to a pillar or woodwork and hang a lantern from the horizontal member. You can stand lights on windowsills or in niches. In a bare modern church you can even run an extending two-inch barrel from floor to ceiling, pack both ends with softboard and then gently screw it tight. If your church has a gallery, you can put lights up there. In the last resort you can simply lay them on the floor. Use your imagination to decide which would be the best method to use in your circumstances. No doubt you will think of many not mentioned here.

At this point you have to decide exactly where you want your lights to be, so first it is useful to consider the various effects of directional lighting. The most obvious place to put the light is IN FRONT, but this is not always as satisfactory as you might expect. Unless the lights are well above the level of the performers' heads, frontal lighting will tend to flatten out their faces. Moreover, it will light the background as well, so that the actors may easily appear camouflaged against a welter of detail behind.

In the ballet, where the human figure is of more importance than the face, a favourite source of lighting is from the SIDE. This leaves the background in comparative darkness, against which the performers stand out brilliantly. It is not quite so good for catching facial expression, but the effect is striking and dramatic. Lighting from BEHIND can be thrilling, even terrifying, but of course you must be careful to keep it out of the audience's eyes. From immediately ABOVE, lights throw the eyes into deep shadow and give a general sense of grimness and foreboding. A single spotlight shining up from BELOW has an effect rather like floats but infinitely more startling. Faces are strangely underlit, and huge shadows race across the walls and roof.

Startling effects of this kind are wanted occasionally, but for most of the time they would be a positive disadvantage. What we need much more often is an effect so natural that nobody in the audience will notice the lighting at all or be aware that it is closing down their area of vision into the narrow compass of the play. How can this be achieved?

In the street, we are used to seeing people lit mainly from above but with plenty of reflection from the ground to soften the shadows. The light is strongest from the direction of the sun, and the opposite side is lit more softly by the general brilliance of the sky. We can imitate this best by setting our lights in two groups, one to the left and one to the right, both well in front of the stage but 45° above the performers and 45° to the side. By a careful balance and subtle colouring, light from these angles can appear so natural as to be almost imperceptible.

To colour our lights, we shall need FILTERS, once known as 'jellies' because they used to be made out of gelatine, but that has long been replaced by more satisfactory materials. These we shall almost certainly have to buy from a specialist firm dealing in theatrical lighting, of which you will find plenty advertised in *Amateur Stage*. Filters are relatively cheap, but remember that they will inevitably flutter down to the ground unless they are held in a FRAME. Each different kind of lantern has its own special frame, which should be supplied with it.

Colour induces mood, and the great temptation for the beginner is to overdo it badly. If the actors are lit scarlet on one side and emerald on the other, this will not necessarily appeal to the emotional depths of your audience; they are more likely to be reminded of a television commercial. Save your surprises for the times when you need them and light the rest of the show to look natural.

For a sunny day, put the colour known as Straw in the lights on one side and Steel Tint on the other. A cosier version of the same effect can be obtained with Pale Gold and Pale Lavender (also known as Surprise Pink), but this will look more like artificial light. If your church runs east and west, it is not a bad idea to put the Straw or Gold on the south side, where the audience is used to seeing sunshine. For night effects you might use Steel Blue (not the Tint this time) juxtaposed with Medium Blue for the shadow side. The merest hint of Pale Amber will give you candlelight, and Orange (not red) is good for fire.

Suppose you are trying to light our imaginary play, *The Prodigal*, which was described in detail in Chapters Six and Seven. You have managed to acquire a small dimmer board with six circuits of 500 watts each, and you have two 500-watt profile spots, three 500-watt Fresnels and two 250-watt floods. Let us put the two profiles out front on either side of the audience and as high as we can reasonably get them, coloured Straw and Steel Tint respectively. These two will be the basis of the 45° 'natural' lighting. Two of the Fresnels are high up on either side of the stage and only just down-stage of it, one coloured Steel Blue, the other Medium Blue. The third Fresnel is down near the floor (remember it can get hot and burn things!) pointing upwards from slightly left of centre and coloured Orange. The two floods are on the ground beyond the choir stalls, pointing at the East End. One is coloured Pale Amber, the other – let's go mad – Peacock Blue.

While the audience is coming in, we will have some light on the stage to make it look different and intriguing. This is called the PRESET. Let us set up as if for night, with the Steel Blue Fresnel at 60% and the Medium Blue at 40%. Try to arrange the houselights so that as little as possible falls on the stage area. We will never sink below this preset at any point during the evening.

As the houselights go out, starting from the back of the nave and working forward towards the acting area (so that the greatest brightness is always near the stage) we bring up the profiles to full on either side. This gives a pleasant daylight effect, with a rather hard, blueish edge from the Fresnels. It is a cold, bright morning on the farm, and the play begins.

Scene Two in the wicked city calls for our most lurid effects, and we are ready with them. As the first scene closes and the characters leave the stage, the two profiles begin to fade down to nil, bringing us back to the night effect of the Preset. We plug the Peacock flood into the dimmer and bring it up to full so as to flood the sanctuary with greenish-blue, switch on the Chinese lantern (remember?) and the new scene begins. Slowly during the action we inch in the third Fresnel, pouring up a fiery glow, which grows brighter and brighter up to the climax, when the Prodigal walks down the steps into the lusciously baited trap. His face is lit as if he stood over a furnace, and behind him his giant shadow stands out in Peacock against a burning sky. After the robbery, the Fresnel fades out again, and he stumbles back into the cold night air of the unfriendly city.

At the end of Scene Two, we had decided for a modified blackout. On the whole, it is a great mistake to attempt a total blackout in church. For one thing you will usually find that streetlights or even moonlight will intrude to spoil it, while your actors and stage staff stumble about into the darkness, bumping into obstacles. But, if we leave the Peacock flood shining on the sanctuary, this will solve both problems at once. It will not really look like a natural night – in this lurid scene it wasn't meant to – but it will cast an eerie luminescence, against which the departing players will appear in silhouette.

For Scene Three, we need the lights to come up to harsh, pitiless daylight. As the Peacock flood begins to fade, on come the Steel Tint profile (out front stage right) and the Steel Blue Fresnel (stage left) both to full. You will need to experiment carefully to find what setting you need for the Medium Blue Fresnel in order to achieve the right effect. The general atmosphere will be in various shades of blue, cold, grim and a touch of nightmare.

Coming back to Scene Four at the farm is easy. You gently fade the two Fresnels back to their original settings as you bring the other front-of-house profile to full. During the scene we quietly unplug the Peacock flood from the dimmer board and replace it with the Pale Amber one. As the party begins, the flood can slowly light up, and perhaps we might check the Straw profile a little bringing up the Steel Blue Fresnel in compensation. Scene Five has a bitter taste, and this colder daylight will reflect it. By contrast, the party seems to be bathed in gold. At the final reconciliation, we might relent a little and bring out the sunlight again, leaving the Father and Son to go in to their happy ending.

Lighting of this kind is not strictly necessary, but it is intended to enhance the emotional impact of the play. That is not to say that the audience should be aware of it. If possible, the only effects they should actually notice are the pyrotechnics of Scene Two. In the other scenes, the lighting plot is aimed not so much at their consciousness as at their instinctive reactions. They should not realise why they feel despairing in Scene Three and instantly reassured in Scene Four, but, if you have got the lighting right, it will have that effect on them. In theory, it is quite possible to make your lighting effects too subtle, but the much more frequent error is to make them too crude.

In church there are also special ways of using light, which have been much explored in *son et lumière*. You can pick out some feature of the building with a narrow shaft of brilliance, you can emphasise the different areas of the church by changes of colour, you can throw light sideways so as to bring the carving into sharp relief. Provided you can arrange some protection from the weather, you can even light a stained-glass window from outside. In a night scene, for instance, it can give a magical effect to see the east window gradually dawn to brightness behind the action.

This is an endless subject, and, if it interests you, there is almost no limit to the effects you can achieve, even with quite limited resources, but do keep a sense of proportion. Nearly forty years ago, a beautiful English translation of a play by a world-famous Frenchman was presented in the West End by a brilliant cast and perhaps the finest director of our century. Coming out of the theatre afterwards, the thing most people picked on was the amazing sunrise in Act Two. Let that be an object lesson, and always remember that the lighting should be the servant of the production, which should not use the play as a pretext for ever more dazzling technical fireworks.

Noises on and off

The use of music and sound is another great enhancement to the emotional impact of a play. This does not only apply to a musical; it can be used with great effect in almost any kind of production. For example you may decide to have music playing when the audience come in, to put them in the mood for the play or simply to make them feel more cosy and comfortable. You may use it during an interval to distract their minds from a scene change. You may even decide to introduce it at some time during the action, possibly in a passage without dialogue.

Noises can be effective too. The crowing of a cock, the tramp of an approaching mob, can have a powerful emotive impact, as well as giving the audience vital information about the story. A church, with its special acoustic properties, can produce very startling effects indeed. There are also ways of changing the quality of the human voice, which have been much exploited by pop groups in recent years. You might perhaps like to have the words of God thundering about the building or whispered like the still, small voice close to the listener's ear.

If it is music you are wanting, then the most obvious available source is the organ. Many churches possess a magnificent instrument, capable of a huge range of sound in pitch, quality and volume. Moreover, the organist is likely to be a competent musician, used to working inside the framework of a service where the music is an integral part of a larger programme. It is very tempting to accept the services of a friendly organist, who will almost certainly be prepared to work with you free of charge.

On the other hand, the organ does present disadvantages. It is designed to fill the church, and, if you are not careful, it can drown your production. More serious, it has a very limited range of moods, especially as the audience will tend to associate it with church services and all that they imply. Suppose you had asked the organist to play suitable music for Scene Two of *The Prodigal* to give the effect of the wicked city. What sort of piece could be played? It would be a brave performer who would attempt rock or ragtime on the organ, and many of the audience might be scandalised to hear it. It is not an easy instrument for rhythm playing, and its effects tend to be grand rather than spare.

Within these limitations, it can be a great help to your show. If, for instance, you are presenting a traditional Passion Play, divided into scenes or stages, there is a great deal of superb organ music written on this theme, stark or rich, according to your taste. The organ can be touching or triumphant, and it has a surprising capacity for horror. Some of the modern French composers make it sound terrifying. A skilled performer with wide-ranging tastes may be able to advise you on the best piece for your needs.

Whatever you do with an organ, it will always sound as if you are in church, whereas the aim of your production may be to carry the audience away to some other place, where the music would sound quite different. In that case, you may do better with other instruments. A pipe of some kind – flute, oboe or even the simple recorder – can create the mountainside for your shepherds, especially if it is played by one of the performers. Drums can provide a mood of menace or even horror, and you can startle your audience with a clash of cymbals. Bells are very evocative and can be played by anyone. There are sheep bells, sleigh bells, church bells and the grim, lonely bell of the leper.

If you want your music to seem part of the play rather than a separate performance on its own, then it is better to avoid instruments that need tuning at the last moment. A piano will only too often give the impression of being outside the action, unless you can find some way of making it and the pianist part of the play. If you are doing a musical, of course, then quite different considerations apply, as the audience will accept any amount of extraneous instruments and tuning up.

The difficulty with all musical instruments is that, unless they are adequately played, they are apt to destroy atmosphere instead of creating it, and comparatively few people are competent instrumentalists these days. Most of those stick to the guitar or drums and play them chiefly as an accompaniment to the human voice.

Rather more people can sing passably than play, and a song, either solo or in chorus, often makes a very effective interlude in the course of the action. Shakespeare made brilliant use of song as a dramatic effect; in their different ways 'Tell me where is fancy bred', Desdemona's 'Willow Song' and Ophelia's mad singing tear our hearts with their drama. Even if your play does not contain a song, you may find a use for one – a ritual Passover Hymn in a play of the Last Supper, a distant chorus of monks in *Murder in the Cathedral*, or even a nightclub singer in the play about the Prodigal. Distant singing, especially in the higher register, can be wonderfully effective in a Gothic church, and the echoing vaults will fill in any thinness of tone.

In many plays there will be moments when the human voice can be used to effect without actually singing. For instance, you can get extraordinary results from humming in different keys. Whistling, too, can be eerie or comic but always evocative. Screams, cries, shouts and distant halloos can all be part of your sound effects, or SFX in stage manager's shorthand. Cries of 'Crucify him!' and 'Barabbas' are sound effects as well as dialogue. In plotting your play, work out where they can be shouted to give the most terrifying effect.

Roaring and shouting will grow tedious if it goes on at one level of decibels for too long. Sound effects need to be orchestrated just like music, not only to be more realistic but to grip your audience by the throat. The sullen murmurs, the crescendo growl like an ominous underswell to Pilate's speech, the occasional cries of angry voices, all leading up to the final roar of 'Barabbas'. Now we know all hope of justice or sanity is lost, and none of the earlier shouts should reach the pitch of that appalling hour.

Actors have hands and feet too, which should be remembered as you plan your sound effects. Hands clapping, or beating on wood or stone, feet shuffling, stamping or tapping a rhythmic beat. Few sounds are more vivid than the clattering echoes of high heels on a stone floor. Naturally, this cuts both ways. Make sure that your cast's footsteps are silent when you want them to be. A secret messenger loses a good deal of his mystery if he clumps his way on stage.

There are also mechanical effects, for instance the thundersheet. This is a large iron sheet, which rumbles when it is shaken. Much beloved in the theatre, they are equally effective in church, but they are dangerous objects and need to be treated with care. Bangs, crashes, rattling chains, hooters, whistles, animal noises – there are any number of possibilities. In one production of *The Way of the Cross* by Henri Ghéon, four actors entered by the west, north, south and east doors of the church, slamming them thunderously behind them after their opening line.

The latest arrivals in the sound effects field are the various forms of electronics, using either microphones or some kind of recorded sound. These can be used for speech, noises or music and possibly for all three at once. Electronic sound can be a wonderful asset to a production, but you will need powerful equipment of high quality if the effect is not to sound tinny in church. It is also vital that the person operating the sound should be completely conversant with the equipment and its potential. It is all too easy to borrow a tape recorder from a kind friend who brings it to the church but can't stay, gets it going in an instant, assures you there are no problems and hurries off again. Ten minutes later it inexplicably stops, and nobody in the group can start it again. It would have been better to settle for something less ambitious which the sound operator knew how to work.

Recordings may be on disc, tape or cassette. RECORD PLAYERS are the least convenient form of recording to use in church. Discs are bulky and easily scratched. It is difficult to lower the needle onto the disc at exactly the point you want, and changing from one disc to another can be a slow and clumsy business. If the sound you want is only on disc, you might be wise to transfer it to a tape, either reel-to-reel or cassette.

Theatres always use REEL-TO-REEL tape recorders. The different sound cues are separately recorded and then joined together with bright lengths of leader tape with the number of the cue marked on the leader. In this way the operator can confidently start the right cue at the exact moment without hesitating for a quarter of a second. If you have the equipment available, this is undoubtedly the best way of doing things. The only trouble is that few homes still have a reel-to-reel recorder, and those that remain are not always in the best of condition.

Finally, there is the CASSETTE PLAYER, which has many advantages. The equipment is fairly compact, and there is no problem with threading a tape. Even so, controls can be very sophisticated these days, so do not assume that anyone can work a strange model at sight. The chief difficulty is that you cannot see where you are on the tape, and few tape counters are accurate enough for your split-second needs. You can of course record each cue on a separate cassette, but it is an expensive way of doing things and means changing the cassette for every single cue.

Besides knowing the machine, the sound operator must also be completely familiar with the play, and if you are doing this job, you should attend as many rehearsals as you can. It is not enough to try and work from a script that you met for the first time at the dress rehearsal. You should know the whole production so well that you can cope with unforeseen emergencies as they arise, and try to develop the sensibility to know when the sound should be louder or softer. Like the other technicians, the sound operator can make or mar the show.

In addition to the player or recorder itself, you will certainly need proper amplification with free-standing LOUDSPEAKERS, if your tape or disc is to give enough sound to fill an average church. The actual placing of loudspeakers needs a good deal of care, and you may decide that you need to put them on extra long leads. For the cast, the most convenient position is behind the stage, especially if they have to dance to recorded music. Trying to keep time to music that the actors cannot hear but the audience can is enough to drive your performers to distraction.

There are other considerations, however. It may be that, if the speakers are behind the stage, they will not be loud enough. Moreover, you may want to startle the audience with a sudden sound from behind them. If you are very well off, you may even decide to have a number of speakers and shift the sound from one to another for different cues or even to achieve effects where the sound seems to swirl past them.

Whatever you decide, and especially if it is ambitious, make sure that all the problems are sorted out at a special technical rehearsal, where all the equipment is set up, all the effects tried and all the snags removed. Electronic sound can be even more time-consuming than lights, so you should not waste everyone's time by struggling with sound effects at the dress rehearsal. Apart from anything else, there is nothing more likely to breed bad feelings between the actors and the backstage staff.

If you are using tracks from commercial records or tapes or cassettes, do remember that they are private property. You have no more right to give a public performance of a track from a record or cassette without permission than you have to perform a play without asking the author or the author's agent. Most sleeves and cassette boxes have a warning to this effect, and they will also give the address of the recording company. In the theatre, all these permissions go through the Performing Rights Society, but you will have to write to the companies individually. Fortunately most of them are very generous and will let you do it for nothing, but you should not bank on that. When writing, explain that it is for a limited number of performances in church, and of course you will have a stronger hand if you can truthfully say you are collecting for charity.

You are not limited to commercial recordings. Perhaps the local school orchestra or some gifted local performer would let you make a recording from them and use it in your play. And music is not the only thing that can be taped. Sound effects such as bird calls, wind, thunder, cartwheels on cobbles, church bells and the like can be recorded live and used as a sound cue.

Remarkable effects can be achieved with the human voice, either recorded or put straight through a microphone. With modern amplifiers, the voice can be altered in very impressive ways. Great volume and a thunderous echo might be your idea of the voice of God. For a really horrifying effect - perhaps Samuel called up by the Witch of Endor - you could even reverse the echo, so that it came before the voice. Try amplifying a whisper or putting a tremolo on ordinary speech, and you may be surprised at the results.

Whatever you decide on, try to bear in mind that all drama is concerned with the unexpected which is also the inevitable. It is excellent that your sound cues should startle the audience, but do make sure that, in retrospect, the reason for them will be seen as clear and right. Don't be tempted to introduce an effect just because you like it; ask yourself whether it is helping the play. Used rightly, sound can add great power to your production; loaded on extravagantly, it can bury your play in a confusing welter of noise.

Drumming up an audience

It is often said of amateur productions, 'Of course they get good audiences because their friends and relatives all turn out to see them.' This is partially true, and particularly so in performances given by children which will be attended by doting parents, sisters, brothers, aunts and cousins. But if your group is putting on a play in a church, and you are all conscious of the power in that play to stir your audience into deeper and profounder thought, you will want to cast your net much wider.

One of the first aids to advertising a play is, of course, the poster. Three points about posters are important:

1 They should look good
2 They should be put up intelligently in places where they will attract attention
3 They should be put up at the right time.

Let's think about these three points. The worst kind of poster is one written out in pale crayon colours with wobbly writing. The best is one that will attract attention across the street, be true to the spirit of the play and give clear and accurate information regarding the time and place of performance. Plan your posters well in advance. Use any influence you may have with a local art school or sixth form art class to get someone to design it for you. It need not be elaborate. But it must be striking. Remember the poster will be the first sight your audience will have of your show. They will make an advance judgement on it just by looking at the printing and illustrations; and, possibly, their decision as to whether or not to come will be influenced by that judgement.

Make sure, in advance, that you have plenty of volunteers to do the foot-slogging work of going round the neighbourhood and putting them up. But make sure beforehand that they are briefed as to where they should be posted. Don't let posters get wasted by putting them on walls where nobody is likely to pass by. Arrange in good time with shops and cafés that they will agree to put them up for you and let your volunteers have the addresses. (Don't forget to offer two complimentary tickets to everyone who allows you to use their premises for this purpose.) And be sure to put them up at the right psychological time. If they go up six weeks before the production, the chances are that people will take notice and then forget about it. If you put them up too late, say ten days to two weeks in advance of your first night, most people will have made other arrangements. It's impossible to make a rule about this as neighbourhoods vary. But the general practice is to have posters up about three weeks before the performance.

Then you must think of how the local clergy will be able to help you. Perhaps the incumbent of the church where you will be perform-ing will agree to alert clergy of all the local churches. In which case, someone should take posters round to them to put up in the church porch or on the noticeboard. It's quite a good idea to have simple handbills printed or duplicated as well. These are smaller and much less costly and you can have hundreds of them run off pretty cheaply. Very often church offices will have someone who will do this for you. Handbills are easy reminders of the time and place of your show. Get all your friends to help with their distribution and even to put them through local letter boxes.

It might be a good idea to write a small piece describing the play and your reasons for putting it on which could be used to insert into church magazines. Perhaps your local press will help you to put some-thing about it in their paper. They will be more ready to do this if you write the 'copy' for them. Had you thought of asking local radio stations to feature your production in a chat show? Though do try to persuade them not to wait till the night of the performance to do this. About a week in advance is possibly the ideal time for this kind of publicity, with a reminder from them on the night that your show will be on that evening.

Then there is the question of making contact with schools, colleges and organisations such as the Mothers' Union or the Women's Institute. The whole question of letting everyone know about your play is one that can involve each member of your group. Ask all those concerned – actors, director, wardrobe, designer, stage managers, lighting team, and all outside helpers – to give you names and addresses of people they know who might be involved in education of one kind or another. Better still, if they will promise to contact these people themselves you will have less work to do. Posters on school or club noticeboards can be helpful. So can publicity put up in the Public Library.

Try to arrange for all the local clergy to give out details about your play in the Sunday notices. Though do try to persuade them not to use that dread phrase, 'We hope you will all come to support this venture . . .' which makes it sound as if the play were something to be endured, and not to be enjoyed. You might ask them to spare the time to read the play beforehand, or perhaps come to a rehearsal. Anything to get your local ministers and priests involved in the excitement which is being generated by your group.

Excitement is catching. Have your group thought of holding a coffee-morning or a wine and cheese party where the forthcoming play could be talked about and guests invited to buy tickets? You could invite key people in your area who would, in their turn, pass on the news to others. People such as school teachers, clergy, journalists, lecturers, leaders of local clubs or Bible study groups, church workers – the list is endless – are all potential supporters of what you are doing. The timing of such an event is important. Possibly about a month before the first night would be an ideal time. You will have plenty to tell them about your production by then, but you won't be plagued by last-rehearsal nerves. Let these key people feel that they are among the first to be given news of your play and try to get them involved with it so that they have a personal sense of identifying with it.

And now we must think of the whole question of tickets for the show. There may well be those in your church who will object to the idea of selling tickets at all, and you will need to respect their feelings. You may have to ask for a retiring collection, or you could sell programmes at the door for the price of a seat. If you are selling tickets, do make sure that they can be bought at least three weeks in advance. Plenty will assure you, 'Oh, I'll come all right, but I will buy at the door.' You will lose a considerable amount of potential audience if you don't sell in advance. Of course people want to come. But the weather may turn rough, they may have a headache, little Tommy may be throwing a tantrum, and the fact that they haven't committed themselves by actually buying a ticket will become an overwhelming inducement for not turning out.

A clergyman friend of ours sold literally hundreds of tickets for a couple of performances at the Round House, London, simply by carrying a book of tickets around with him and asking everyone with whom he came into contact to buy one. Try to persuade everyone connected with your play to do the same. Once people have bought tickets they will make every effort to come, despite weather, headache or difficult children!

It's a useful idea to appoint someone to be in charge of the selling of tickets whose responsibility will be to account for all tickets (or programmes) sold or distributed and to collect the money. The same person might also undertake to arrange for a box office. This should preferably be either in a house or office where someone is available to answer the telephone most of the time. Sometimes a local shop will be willing to take on the job of selling your tickets for you. Details of where tickets can be bought or if there is to be a retiring collection should be on the poster.

The keynote to drumming up an audience is your own enthusiasm for the play and your faith in what it is saying. Your group will have chosen the play for its ability to illumine some aspect of human life, and because they feel that the spirit of Christ is breathing through it. So don't let this initial response to the play become dimmed by too many personal concerns such as the director's 'Will my reputation be increased by this production?'; or the actor's 'What will people think about my performance?'; or the designer's 'I hope everyone will remark on the brilliance of my colour-schemes.' Of course all those concerned with the play should be doing their best, but their hearts and wishes should be set on what the play, as a whole, is saying both to them and to their audiences.

This enthusiasm and faith in the play will infect everyone who is told about it, and they will *want* to come.

EIGHTEEN

On the night

Up till now your group will have been concerned with the play; with the actors, the director, the designer, the stage management, and with the intricate jig-saw of putting the whole together. But now the first night has arrived and you have a new concern on your hands. After all, though you may have forgotten it in the confusion of cues, costumes, props and sets, your audience is your *first* concern. They are the very reason why the play has been put on. And it's all too easy to forget their needs in the nerves and excitements of the production itself.

First and foremost, they should feel welcomed. Think for a moment of the evening from their point of view – it's a dirty night and they have made a special effort to turn out; they have had to wait in the rain at the bus-stop, or on a draughty platform for a train; they have found at the last moment that the car battery has failed; they arrive at the church (perhaps they have never been inside a church before); and if there is some friendly person at the door to make them feel welcomed, the discomforts are soon forgotten. But if, when they have struggled to find out which of the church doors is the actual entrance there is nobody there to take their dripping umbrella; if the place is so unheated that they sit shivering in a damp coat; then it's small wonder if they privately decide never to come to such an event again.

Never forget that the audience has paid to watch the performance not only with money, but (and this is far more valuable), with their time and attention. This is why your 'Front of House' arrangements should never be neglected. 'But this is not a theatre', you may protest, 'so why should it be so important?' It's just because your play is in a church that you should give very careful attention to making your audience as comfortable as possible. Christians haven't always the reputation of loving their neighbour. They are accused of being stand-offish and cliquey. If you are to attract the non-believers into the church for your performance and to hope that they will come again and, possibly, even come back to a service there, it will be a poor look-out for them if there is no one to give them a smile when they arrive, to sell them a programme and show them to a seat. All these are elementary courtesies in any theatre and should not be omitted just because your production is in a church.

You will need a HOUSE MANAGER whose job it will be to co-ordinate ushers, programme sellers and refreshments. The house manager is the one who should welcome the audience as they come in. If tickets are sold at the door, the house manager will need to find someone to act as box office for the evening. Whoever looks after the box office (usually a simple table at the entrance to the building), should be prepared for occasional arguments about tickets and seats and keep even-tempered throughout. Programme sellers can often double as ushers, as they do in many theatres, and they should be provided with plenty of small change beforehand together with a purse to keep it in, preferably one which can be slung round the neck, or on a belt.

Programmes need not be elaborate, but they should be clear. Dupli-cated A4 folded in half make a good-sized programme. Don't forget to mention your technical helpers as well as your actors and director on the programmes. And why not add your front of house helpers as well? Anything you can do to give the whole of your group a sense of being part of a team, the more warm and contented the atmosphere of your production will be. And don't forget to acknowledge anyone who has lent furniture or given help in any particular way.

Then there is the question of refreshments. These are all a part of your welcome and should always be provided in some form to give your audience a chance to talk to each other and, in particular, to those who may have come to the church for the first time. Some groups like to greet their audience with something hot if it's a winter night. Others plan a buffet supper for after the performance. The most usual practice is to provide tea or coffee during the interval. This gives people a chance to walk about and stretch their legs after sitting in hard chairs or uncomfortable pews. There is the kind of Christian who is apt to tell you not to serve refreshments 'because you shouldn't let worldly considerations stand in the way of the play's message'. These high-minded souls quite forget that Jesus himself fed the multi-tude after he had been preaching to them. The first thing he said after the raising of Jairus' daughter from death was 'Give her to eat'. After all, the sacrament of Holy Communion sprang from an evening meal. Do make sure that the coffee is good coffee and that everything is served attractively. Of course you will need a separate set of helpers for this who will also need to be made to feel a part of the whole. Washing up after the performance can be less of a chore if the connection between it and the play can be established beforehand. One small note here to these very helpers. Rattling cups just before the end of the first act can be dreadfully disturbing both to the audience and to the actors on stage. It's better to keep the audience waiting a moment or two for their tea or coffee than to begin preparations that involve making a noise. This applies to after the interval just as much. All washing up should be left till the play is over.

Do try to persuade your vicar or minister to make your performance in the church something in which all the regular church-goers are involved. If the church as a whole can play 'host' to the rest of your audience, the welcome will be even wider. Ask each church member to look out for someone to talk to whom they don't already know. They may be members of other denominations. They may be complete strangers. But if they find the church people friendly their enjoyment of the evening will be far greater than if they are left to drink their cup of tea in isolation or are talked across by two people who know each other.

Make sure that the church is kept at a comfortable temperature for your audience. If it's a hot summer day open all the windows well beforehand: you may have to close them when the play begins. If the weather is wintry make sure that the heating is turned on early in the day. A few electric fires switched on half an hour before the arrival of the audience may leave them shivering in their overcoats.

Finally, there is the question of the company itself. Your director will take care to control justifiable anxieties and be at hand to encourage the cast and help to assure them that all will be well. This is not the moment for giving any notes except general ones such as: 'Remember your consonants' or 'Don't drop your eyes on the floor'. Notes can be given after a first performance in which case it's best to wait till the next day before giving them.

Perhaps the wardrobe assistant could be given the task of making sure that there are adequate dressing-rooms for the cast. Usually churches run to two vestries – one for the incumbent, and one for the choir; so it's not difficult to have separate rooms for the men and the women of the company. Wardrobe will need to make sure that tables are protected by clean paper, that the lighting is bright enough (anglepoise lamps make the ideal lighting for non-theatre dressing-rooms), that there are good mirrors, that there are washing facilities and a nearby WC. Hanging space is usually available in cupboards containing clergy and choir robes.

The stage manager should be clear about cues between the stage and the front of house, and should contact the front of house manager well in advance to establish cues for beginning the show and each subsequent act.

Finally, wherever possible, suggest that there should be a moment when all those taking part in the evening – actors, director, stage-management, front of house, lighting and sound technicians, the wardrobe assistants, and those helping with the refreshments, should join together in a brief moment of prayer. This will have to be before the audience come in and be a private affair, and no doubt either the vicar or minister or someone from the company will lead it. This will help to quieten nerves, still frayed tempers and to remind everyone of the underlying purpose of the play.

Where do we go from here?

Suddenly it's all over, and normal life seems rather flat. For weeks all your energies have been devoted to the great event - the careful preparations, the gathering pace, the final moment of the first night with its inevitable disappointments as well as triumphs - and where has it all gone? A week later it is quite hard to believe that there ever was a play at all.

There is, of course, the clearing up to be done. The stage will have to be dismantled, the lighting returned to its owners (cables conscientiously wound) and all the costumes and props stored away. One job that will have to be faced sooner or later is that of returning the borrowed damask tablecloth back to its owner and pointing out that frightful stain in the corner where someone spilt black coffee during a rehearsal. Of course we shall have to get it laundered, but it's better to own up at once. It is courteous to write letters of thanks to all those who have helped from outside the group - the shop which acted as a booking office, the group who organised refreshments and, above all, the church council who contributed some of the money.

All these things will keep us busy, but they don't hold out much future. The question now is 'What are we going to do next?'

If you feel brave enough, it is not a bad thing to hold a post mortem on the production to discover where things went wrong. This can be a delicate business - you may be surprised to find out how easily your own feelings can be hurt, and others are just as sensitive. A good idea is to plan it in two stages. For a start, hold an internal meeting of your whole team - director, actors, stage staff, designer and wardrobe - to exchange impressions. Up till now the director has been the unquestioned leader, but for this meeting you will learn most if everyone feels free to speak openly. The aim is not so much to criticise one another as to find out where people felt unhappy or were in difficulties. There may have been times when an actor didn't fully understand what the director was asking for; perhaps the assistant stage manager has thought of a better way of hanging a light, but in the last-minute rush nobody would listen.

Following on the meeting (and provided you are all still friends!), you might try a second one that would include the clergy, the church council and anyone who may have taken a particular interest in the production or helped with front-of-house jobs. Again there is always the risk of feelings being hurt, but you can also learn a lot from the candid comments of outsiders. The purpose of both meetings is not so much to allot praise or blame as to pool the information you need for planning what to do next. The sort of questions that need to be asked at this second meeting are: did we get as many people as we hoped for? why did some come and others stay away? was the publicity reaching the right targets? did people feel that the play was suitable for the church? did they enjoy it when they came? do they feel it has added to their Christian insights? were the front-of-house arrangements satisfactory? could everybody see and hear? were they too cold, too hot, uncomfortable? were they shocked, or bored or bewildered? You may have to ask these questions to get the members of your meeting talking. Most of us feel rather diffident when faced with the question: 'Now, have you any criticism of this play?' But if we are asked specific questions, we may feel brave enough to out with the truth.

All truths should be welcome, whether or not they are attractive, and if you receive no criticism at all, it may seem that you are very lucky or have not encouraged people to speak their minds.

On the basis of what they tell you, and including the opinions voiced by members of your group in the first meeting, you can begin to plan for the future.

It may be that your play has been so much of a success that it seems a pity to scrap it altogether. Have you considered the possibility of taking it 'on tour' to other churches in your area? If the group likes the idea, you will need to contact surrounding clergy (some of whom may have been to your production) to find out if any of them would like to invite you to their churches. If they do, that is very encouraging, but of course it will present you with a number of practical problems. Another church may be totally different from the church you have been working in and will provide you with a new set of obstacles and opportunities. Before accepting such an invitation the director and stage manager would be wise to make a careful reconnaissance of the new building and work out the changes that would be necessary to bring the production there.

Rehearsals will have to be called again to incorporate the necessary adjustments in the way of staging, lighting and the placing of furniture and props.

You will need to discuss the terms on which you are coming. Can you afford to offer the show gratis? Are you asking for expenses? Will you take a collection? Whatever the arrangement, you will have to depend on your hosts for publicity and front-of-house assistance, so all details should be clearly settled well beforehand.

Touring a play in this way is a very different matter from the gathering tension of the first night. Your group has given up precious free time for the original production but they can hardly be expected to keep up that kind of pressure indefinitely. Inevitably the new rehearsals will lack some of the excitement of the earlier ones, and dates and times for them should be cleared well in advance and stuck to. One touring performance a month will probably involve you in quite a lot of work; two is probably the maximum in the early stages. Every time you take the play into a new church and adapt it to the building you will be learning more and more about the possibilities of your group as well as adding to its reputation.

Whether you decide to continue with the old production or to discard it, the time has already come to be thinking about the next show. For one thing, you are at an ideal moment for recruiting new members. Quite a number of those who came to see your play may have been inspired by an impulse to join in, and you need to have something to offer them now. Naturally it doesn't have to be a full-scale production, especially for the newcomers. Sketches for church or street, workshops or theatre games will give them plenty of occupation and allow you to discover their abilities.

Unless you are very easily discouraged, you will, however, want to launch out on another play in the not-too-distant future. One question will be: 'How soon?' There is no general answer, but it is possible to set limits of a kind. Don't wait much longer than a year. Memories are short, and you don't want to lose the momentum of your previous show. If people enjoyed it last time, they are all the more likely to come again.

On the other hand, you will make even more problems for yourselves by trying to do anything too soon. Your group has its own private life to lead, and many of them will welcome the opportunity to give more time to their domestic responsibilities. A play takes anything up to three months to rehearse, after which most of them will want some time off with their families or friends. There is the audience to be considered as well. You don't want them to be saying, 'Oh, not another play!' For the moment, it might be best to set an outside limit of two plays a year. Later, when your company has grown larger and casts and directors can be alternated, you might feel able to raise the number to three or even four.

Whatever happens, you don't want to lower your standards by putting on too many plays. It's a temptation to think that if the play is Christian then that, in itself, is good enough, and we don't have to bother too much about standards. It is just *because* the play is Christian that it should be the very best that we can offer. If our drama is for God and for our neighbour we must be careful not to short-change either.

So what do we do next time? Perhaps your first play was chosen for being easy and simple, so you may want to try something more ambitious. Was the last show just a little too much over the heads of your audience? Perhaps the next production could be more straight-forward. Was it controversial? Then possibly the next one could be traditional. Don't brush aside the comments of your audience. You do not need to compromise your artistic or dramatic integrity to please them, but if you fail to touch them they won't come back again and you will have failed altogether.

Whatever choice you make, your group is beginning to grow into a continuing team rather than an experimental 'scratch' side, and you will begin to live with some of the responsibilities that go with this change. Money for example: you may have made something out of your last show, so now you will be deciding what to do with it. This is a decision which the whole group should take together. Perhaps you will want to repay the generous grant from the church committee (not forgetting that they will be the more likely to be generous next time), perhaps you will decide to give some of it to a charity, or to the church funds. You will probably need to keep some as seedcorn for the next production, and in that case you will need a treasurer to look after it.

On the other hand, you may have run into debt, in which case you may be thinking of holding coffee mornings, or a car boot sale to raise the necessary funds, and someone will have to be in charge of this.

As the group grows and flourishes, it will inevitably begin to assume the aspect of an institution. You may find yourselves electing a committee to choose scripts, to appoint directors and to cope with all the problems that beset any amateur dramatic society which is succeeding. This kind of organisation can be of great assistance to your group, but it can also tend to damp down creativity. Beware of the committee whose members are unwilling to resign after a few years, of the power complex which bedevils the very best of Christian organisations, of prejudice against change in any form.

Never lose sight of the truth that drama is about people, about finding them fascinating without condemnation, about loving without being sentimental, about the joy of getting out of ourselves in order to understand others.

So, accept change where it is for the better, welcome new blood into your group, be on the alert against forming cliques; and work as hard as you can to make your audience glad they made the effort to leave their comfortable firesides to come and see your play.

Appendix
Voice Drama

Voice dramas should be spoken (either read or learnt by heart) by a group; or they can be spoken by one group and mimed by another; or, more ambitiously, the voice drama can be both spoken and acted by one group only.

The voice drama can be used in workshops or for performance during a church service. This particular voice drama is based on the story of Jairus' daughter (Mark 5.22-43)

There Was Always The Crowd

There was always the crowd,
chatting, excited, waiting for Jesus to walk down the street -
waiting for a sight of his face,
the sound of his voice -
waiting for him to change their lives
and the lives of others -
waiting, hoping - waiting for a miracle.

Some of them were young, noisy, waving their hands,
shouting.
Some were old and quiet, walking with difficulty,
frightened of falling down.
Some were crippled.
Some ill with fevers.
Some blind.
One of them was a woman who had been bleeding for twelve years.
She had no money left because she had given it all to the doctors
who had taken it - 'Thank you' - but they had failed to heal her.

One was an important man, Jairus, a ruler of the people,
whose daughter was very ill - very *very* ill.

Jairus came through the crowd to Jesus.
An important man like Jairus doesn't have to push.
The crowd parted to let him through.

'Master, my little daughter is ill, very *very* ill.
If only you would come to my house she might be cured.'

The crowd began to talk.
'Will he go?'
'Will the child get healed?'
'I wanted him to cure me first.'
'He mustn't be allowed to go away from us!'
'Cure *me*, Lord Jesus!'
The woman with the bleeding caught hold of Jesus' robe
                                    as he was turning to follow Jairus.

Jesus looked round: 'Who touched me?'

Peter and James were there and they said, 'Master, the crowd is
                                    pressing in on every side,
how can you ask such a question?'
And the crowd repeated, 'How could you ask such a question?'

But the woman knew he had sensed her urgent need.
She also knew that she was healed.
'Master, I caught hold of your robe. I couldn't let you go before
                                    you had cured me.
And, look at me! I am well now!'
The woman knelt at his feet and kissed them.
And Jesus said to her,
'Daughter, go in peace, your faith has healed you.'

Then came a new commotion.
'Make way for the servant of the Lord Jairus!'
Someone was pushing his way through the crowd.
'Careful!' 'Look where you're going!'
But the man was in a hurry and he took no notice of them.
He ran to Jairus, 'My lord! My lord! I bring dreadful news!'
The crowd drew closer to hear what he had to say.
Jesus waited.
Jairus knew what the news must be. He said nothing.
'It is too late for the Master to come and heal her. It is too late.'
The servant was weeping. The crowd began to weep.
Jairus stood still.
The little girl was his only child.
He simply stood there like a man of wood.

Jesus went up to him. 'Do not be afraid, Jairus, my friend.
'Only believe that God will heal her and she shall be made whole.'

So Jairus led the Master to his house, with the servant following.
And the crowd following.
And Peter and James.
The servant wept.
The crowd wept.
And from inside the house came the cries of lamentation for the
                              dead child.
The noise was very loud indeed.

Jesus lifted up his hands to silence them.
'Do not make all this noise for a little girl who is asleep.'
And they laughed at him. Laughed. Laughed. Laughed.
But then kept quiet.
'Where is the mother of the child?'
Jairus took his wife by the hand and brought her to the Master.
'Let the father and mother of the little girl come with me into the room,
and you, Peter; and you, James. The rest must remain outside.'

It was very still in the room now. The only movement was the
                              flickering of candles beside the child.
The yellow flames flickered and danced.
But the little girl on the bed lay like an unlit candle still as wax.

Peter and James bowed their heads and prayed.
The mother and father of the child prayed as best they could.
All of them tried to believe as the Master had taught them.
But Jesus went to the bed as if he was about to wake the little
                              girl from a natural sleep.
He took her hand and spoke to her,
'Little girl, get up. It is time for you to wake!'
No more than that. It was all so simple.

They saw the little girl's hand grow warm to clasp the hand of Jesus.
They saw how life came back into her cheeks, how her mouth broke
                              into a smile.
They saw, and tried to believe that they, too, were not asleep.
But when she sat up in the bed and said, 'I am so hungry!'
they ran to her and put their arms round her and kissed her.
But Jesus knew that the little girl needed food more than kisses
                              at that moment.
'Give her some lunch,' he said.

It was all so simple for him. So ordinary.
'And don't go around talking about what's happened,'
he cautioned them.

How could they help talking? To them it was a miracle,
something they could only believe because they had seen it happen.

How do *you* feel about it?
You in the crowd?
Would you go around talking?
Or would you obey the Master and keep silent?
Would you believe it happened had you not been there yourself?
Would you believe even if you had?
Do you believe now?

Further Reading

Books on Religious Drama

Browne, E. Martin. *Two in One*, Cambridge University Press, 1981

Bucknell, Peter E. *Entertainment and Ritual*, London, Stainer & Bell, 1979

Edwards, Francis. *Ritual Drama*, Cambridge, Lutterworth, 1976

Grainger, Roger. *Presenting Drama in Church*, London, Epworth, 1985

Grinham, Gillian. *Know How to Use Drama in Church*, London, Scripture Union, 1979

Pickering, Kenneth W. *Drama in the Cathedral*, Sussex, Churchman, 1984

Robins, Carina. *Drama for God*, London, S.C.M. Press, 1977

Stagecraft

Baker, Hendril. *Stage Management and Theatre Craft* (3rd edn), Worcester, J. Garnet Miller, 1981

Bowskill, Derek. *Acting and Stagecraft Made Simple*, London, W. H. Allen, 1979

Fernald, John. *The Play Produced*, London, Kenyon-Deane, 1952

Legat, Michael. *Putting On a Play*, London, Robert Hale, 1984

Miller, James Hull. *Technical Aspects of Staging in the Church*, London, Stacey, 1977

Richmond, Susan. *A Text Book of Stagecraft* (current edn), London, Kenyon-Deane, 1981

Richmond, Susan. *Further Steps in Stagecraft*, London, Kenyon-Deane, 1983

Lighting

Bentham, Frederick. *The Art of Stage Lighting*, London, Pitman, 1970

Reid, Francis. *Stage Lighting Handbook* (2nd edn), London, A & C Black, 1982

Acting and Speech

Berry, Cicely. *Voice and the Actor*, London, Harrap, 1973

Berry, Cicely. *Your Voice and How to Use It*, London, Harrap, 1975

Colson, Greta. *Drama Skills*, London, Barrie & Jenkins, 1980

Gondon, W. R. and Mammen, E. W. *The Art of Speaking Made Simple*, London, W. H. Allen, 1980

Hodgson, John and Richards, Ernest. *Improvisation*, London, Methuen London, 1966

Miles-Brown, Johnny. *Acting*, London, Peter Owen, 1985

Rich, Kathleen. *The Art of Speech: A Handbook of Elocution*, Henley-on-Thames, Gresham, 1978

Costume

Brooke, Iris. *English Costume of the Early Middle Ages*, London, A & C Black, 1936

Ingham, Rosemary, and Covey, Elizabeth. *The Costume Designer's Handbook*, Hemel Hempstead, Prentice-Hall, 1983

Kelly, Marie. *On English Costume*, London, Kenyon-Deane, 1931

Oxenford, Lyn. *Design for Movement* (2nd edn), Worcester, J. Garnet Miller, 1983

Makeup

Buchman, Herman. *Stage Makeup*, London, Pitman, 1979

Other

Barker, Clive. *Theatre Games*, London, Methuen London, 1977

Govier, J. *Create Your Own Stage Props*, London, A & C Black, 1984

Morris, Desmond. *Manwatching*, London, Cape, 1977

Napier, Frank. *Curtains for Stage Settings* (2nd edn), Worcester, J. Garnet Miller, 1949

Pease, Allan. *Body Language*, London, Sheldon, 1981

Southern, Richard. *Stage Setting*, London, Faber & Faber, 1937

Useful Addresses

RADIUS (The Religious Drama Society of Great Britain), St Paul's Church, Covent Garden, Bedford Street, London WC2E 9ED.
Tel: 01-836 8669
To make full use of this society, it is necessary to become a member, but the subscription is moderate. They have an extensive library of plays and books on drama. As a member, you can borrow individual titles free and hire play sets at very reasonable charges. They hold a regular annual summer school and other occasional courses.

British Theatre Association
(formerly British Drama League)
9 Fitzroy Square, London W1P 6AE
Tel: 01-387 2666
Once again, it is worth joining the association if you want to make use of it. Like RADIUS, they allow members to borrow titles and hire play sets. Their library (The British Theatre Play Library) is very large indeed, but only part of it is going to be much use for plays in church. They run almost continuous training courses in all aspects of theatre, but of course they are not specifically directed at church groups.

National Association of Drama Advisers
c/o Geoff Malbon, Drama Adviser, Advisers Office, Derbyshire College of Higher Education, Chatsworth Hall, Matlock, Derbyshire
Tel: 0629-3411 Ext 6590
They can put you in touch with your local drama adviser, if you have one, but they are an endangered species. If not already extinct in your area, the drama adviser exists to help drama with advice, information, loans of equipment, contacts and even occasionally a little money.

The Performing Rights Society Ltd
29/33 Berners Street, London W1P 4AA
Tel: 01-580 5544
Every time you play a record or a cassette tape as part of a public performance, you probably owe money to this society. If you do not tell them, you may get away with it, but how do you feel about that? You will find them quite human and sympathetic.

Theatre Roundabout Ltd
859 Finchley Road, London NW11 8LX
Tel: 01-455 4752
This is our own two-person company, on whose experience this book has been based. In addition to presenting professional performances in churches, halls and theatres, we can also offer workshops lasting two hours, half a day, a whole day or an entire weekend, teaching up to 40 people and preparing them for dramatic interludes to be presented in church.
(Similar recommended groups include Footprints and the justly celebrated Riding Lights. Further details about these and other professional companies can be obtained from RADIUS.)

Important Publishers
Catalogues available from:
Samual French Ltd
52 Fitzroy Street, London W1P 6JR
Tel: 01-387 9373
Mainly West End successes, but they have a separate section of religious drama.
Methuen London Ltd
11 New Fetter Lane, London EC4P 4EE
Tel: 01-583 9855
Enormous and fascinating play-list, though they do not reckon themselves religious.
Faber & Faber Ltd
3 Queens Square, London WC1N 3AU
Tel: 01-278 6881
Smaller list but more religious work. For instance, they do all T. S. Eliot.
RADIUS (for address see above)
Very small list of titles but all aimed at church groups and all modern.
Stacey Publications
1 Hawthorndene Road, Hayes, Bromley, Kent BR2 7D2
Tel: 01-462 6461
They publish *Amateur Stage* and other interesting publications.
J. Garnet Miller Ltd
311 Worcester Road, Malvern, Worcs WR14 1AN
Tel: 06845-65045
Small specialists in religious plays for amateurs.
National Christian Education Council
Robert Denholm House, Nutfield, Surrey RH1 4HW
Tel: 682-2411
Kenyon-Deane Ltd
129 St John's Hill, London SW11 1TD
Tel: 01-223 3472